F☉CUSED
AND
INSPIRED

Keeping Our Athletes Safe in a Win-at-All-Costs World

Lisa Mitzel

ISBN-13: 978-1724242792
ISBN-10: 1724242792

 Designs for Wellness Press
P.O. Box 1144
Prosper, TX 75078-1144
DesignsForWellnessPress.com

First edition, September 2018

LISA MITZEL
REACH · SWEAT · BELIEVE
LisaMitzel.com

Cover design by George Foster
FosterCovers.com

Cover illustration by Maryna Voloshyna

 Book designed by Judi Eichler Design Studio
JudiEichlerDesigns.com

Praise for Focused and Inspired

"A revolutionary book that answers the urgent call to identify and prevent abuse in sports. Lisa Mitzel inspires us to embrace wisdom, positive partnerships, and truly value the athlete's voice, daily, on the path to success."
—Steve Kerr, Three-time NBA Champion Head Coach, Golden State Warriors

"Lisa is a beautiful and eloquent writer, whose message speaks loudly through her insight and years of experience. This book tackles not just the important issue of safety in sports, but also transcends safety in today's human culture. A must-read for everyone."
—Marcia Frederick, 1st Female World Gymnastics Champion, Olympian, Gymnastics Hall of Fame, Congressional Medal recipient, Sister Survivor of Abuse, Safety Advocate

"Developing athletes with emotional intelligence is not only wise, but necessary for athletes' health and well-being. In *Focused and Inspired*, Lisa illuminates the crucial topic of safety in sports and shows us that young athletes feel pressured, overwhelmed, and don't have the ability to identify abuse. Children are not merely small adults. It's time for the sports world to pay attention—this vital education is for you."
—Sally S. Harris, MD, MPH, Pediatric and Adolescent Sports Medicine Specialist, Departments of Sports Medicine, Palo Alto Medical Foundation

"As an international coach dealing with many cultures, I look for the edge in ways to educate our coaches and heighten our team's performance. Lisa's insights are powerful! From *Focused and Inspired*, I am now more aware of the psychological needs of our athletes, how coaches can affect them, and how we can integrate joint mental strategies to build confidence and increase winning. Thank you, Lisa!"
—Ricardo Azevedo, 3-Time Olympic Water Polo Coach, Technical Director & National Teams Coordinator, Brazilian Federation

"When people feel unsafe, they simply can not be their best. With *Focused and Inspired*, Lisa Mitzel has created a valuable resource for coaches to help their athletes feel safe and powerful so they can aspire to be all they can be—as Better Athletes, as Better People."
—Jim Thompson, Founder/CEO Positive Coaching Alliance, Author, *Elevating Your Game: Becoming a Triple-Impact Competitor*

"Lisa Mitzel is a true leader and is now sparking a new culture in sports: Thoughts and feelings matter. In this must-read book, Lisa sheds light on how communication affects athletes, daily, and that coaches can evolve and win more through awareness and higher-mind thinking."
—Scott Johnson, 1984 Olympic Gold Medalist and 1988 Olympic Team Captain, Owner and Coach of Scott Johnson's Tumble & Gymnastics Academy

"In sports, it's vital to teach athletes how to communicate with a high level of trust and honesty regarding fear, bullying, intimidation, or even sexual abuse. In *Focused and Inspired*, Lisa gives us the tools to increase athlete safety by communicating positively, effectively, and with empathy to help athletes face hard issues. Education is the key and this book is a must-read for every coach and parent."
—Steve Arkell, USA & Canada National Team Coach, USA Gymnastics National Staff, Head Coach, Maverick's Gymnastics
—Gaby Arkell, Junior Olympic and Elite Coach, Maverick's Gymnastics

To every athlete who has ever been abused
through the misuse of power in sports:
You matter, your voice matters, and we are listening.
This book is especially dedicated to the athlete-survivors of sexual abuse
who are still healing, and who shared their stories and pain.
You are incredibly brave.
Thank you for helping others speak up. Thank you, forever.

For my dad, Jim Mitzel,
who taught, supported, cheered for, and protected all seven of us kids.
You made us laugh, and you gave the best biggest hugs at the front door
when you came home. Thanks for helping me reach my dreams, Dad,
and for showing me great compassion for others and absolute integrity.
Your humility and ability to evolve are amazing examples for us all.

Table of Contents

Foreword

I saw an angel in the marble
so I carved and carved
until she was set free…
~Michelangelo, 1498 A.D.

There is something quite magical about our collective human spirit. Even in its darkest hour, the seed for success against all odds secretly looms just beneath the surface. When we as a society stumble and begin to fall, along come truly talented individuals within its own ranks who courageously rise up at precisely the right time to catch us.

Lisa Mitzel is clearly one of these innovative leaders who boldly clears a path in this complex and often murky world of sport. Her purpose and messages are not only universally important for mental and emotional well-being, but necessary for the safety of our athletes. In her latest book entitled *Focused and Inspired,* Lisa confronts the pervasive lack of emotional intelligence, power issues, and athlete abuse head-on. She provides effective, workable solutions which positively impact virtually all athletes, parents, and coaches in every sport activity.

Focused and Inspired brings to the table a missing dimension in the teaching and training of young athletes—one that is person-centered—and facilitates excellence through a 'power balance' among coaches, parents and their athletes. Lisa inspires us with her 'partnership' model, how to create meaningful human connections, and the practice of open, active, and transparent communications. Her seemingly simplistic insights connecting these players-on-stage house a unique social perspective and a "can-do" attitude that represents a major breakthrough in the field of sports coaching. Using higher-mind thinking and comprehensive strategies for success, Lisa demonstrates why a sincere, positive working synergy is the basis for intrinsic motivation, and attaining peak performances in sports.

> To all coaches out there, I say, "If you have a goal greater than yourself, then listen to and welcome the wisdom in this book."

> To all parents of young athletes, I say, "If you truly want the very best outcomes for your athletes, then listen to and practice the patient communication in this book."

> And to all those aspiring young athletes I say, "If you really seek to know the true meaning of winning, then listen carefully to what Lisa has to say."

If ever there was a need-fulfilled, it can be found in Lisa Mitzel's ground-breaking new book, *Focused and Inspired*.

Gerald S. George, Ph.D.
USA Gymnastics Hall of Fame

INTRODUCTION
Hey! I'm Right Here!
Athletes are people, no matter how small!

Helloooo! This book is a shout to coaches, parents, and leaders all over the world! Because guess what, we are in the thick of an evolution. With the current abuse and safety issues in the sports world, what has become very clear is a need for a universal acceptance of the highest truth: What matters *most* is an athlete's safety and well-being. Not winning. Safety and well-being is *it*, which means mental and emotional health. So, let's take a breath…The sports world has been shaken up, and gosh darn it, we're all in this together. We've been hearing from hundreds of brave athletes about verbal, emotional, physical, and sexual abuse. They're telling us harsh and affecting stories. And now we recognize that *while training, in every sports program in the country,* the highest priority must be their mental and emotional well-being. Every. Single. Athlete.

Athletes are vulnerable: they don't want to make a mistake, they don't want to make their coach mad, they don't want to let down their team-mates or disappoint their parents. The worst one…athletes don't want to be viewed as "weak." Competing in a sport is about being strong, tough, able to endure—and going for the win. So, inside every athlete, nervousness, anxiety, and fear are commonplace. And adults have all the power.

With mounds of talent in sport, and incredibly tough athletes (who are like superheroes), we cannot dismiss that athletes have *emotions*, and in fact, they have *essential* mental and emotional needs. If you want "success" for your athlete, if you want to have a healthy and happy athlete,

 this book will be essential for *you*. As you dive into each chapter, the urgent topics are *not* skill-oriented, they are people-oriented. I teach and speak about the interior, the intrinsic—the inside of physical performance—like self-awareness, emotional intelligence, positive communication, and feelings of personal safety. Because the mind and body work together. Coaches and athletes have followed decades of a "work tradition," and I've been part of that. But today, we are seeing terrible problems and emotional pain. The tradition is *not* working. It's now time for change.

We can coach and motivate in a healthy way *and succeed*. We can create great partnerships with athletes. In a "partnership" we connect deeply. We observe, discuss, ask, and listen to athletes, loudly. This partnership begins with authentic human connection—and it's meaningful. In sport, human connection is not the icing… it's the cake! Welcome the athletes' thoughts and feelings. Collaborate and unite as one!

That doesn't mean we can't be firm, push, and encourage. No. It's sports. Kids need to line-up, pay attention, be efficient, face challenges, and learn to be resilient. But where the traditional coach-mindset was to take command, "do it right," "win at all costs," and develop tough kids, we have actually lost. It hit us hard with the 2017 sexual abuse case with the Olympic doctor and hundreds of female athletes spoke up. We were shocked—by both the abuse and that no one listened, cared enough, or took action. The root problem? *The way we think and treat athletes in sports.* Athletes have been yelled at, isolated, emotionally affected, and psychologically diminished. Instead of "power-over," we need to create a *power balance.* We can listen to each athlete and work together. Listen to their voices. For the smallest of small, it is our job to protect, and in that process, athletes deserve and need to be heard.

If you haven't read Dr. Seuss' *Horton Hears a Who!* recently, you may want to find a copy and dig in. This is a story about safety and equality. It's about the littlest, seemingly insignificant people, and not *hearing* their voices. It is profound. At one peak crisis moment, all the tiny Whos in Whoville are about to get boiled in oil, so they holler, shout, scream, and make noise. They whoop, rattle, ring bells, and blast toots. And finally, finally, the smallest Who cries out a resounding "YOPP!!!" and they are heard…and saved.

We can learn from Dr. Seuss. We can listen to the small people—the athletes. The reason for this book, *Focused and Inspired,* is to teach and instill new awareness, and safety—the value of listening to athletes, and how to let their experience steer the learning process and ensure success. When we learn the nuances of effective communication and positive motivation, when we listen to athletes and look into their eyes with genuine care and curiosity—we are better. We can do what's morally right: be kind and respectful and win at the same time.

To create change, and build a new culture in sports, I am speaking up and joining the athletes triggered by the horrifying 2017 sexual abuse case in the sports world. We have watched, read, and heard of so many problems because of money, power, egos, and making winning the top priority. In the NCAA, USOC, and in practically every U.S.A. sport organization, there are politics, abuse of some kind, and even extortion. It's vital we go back to basics. Let's focus on the values in sports and education. Treasure the athletes' growth and personal triumphs, and express that deep sense of humility when it's our turn to win.

Anyone who supports, cares for, or works with athletes and young people can learn and benefit from this book, including:

- Coaches at every level, in every sport

- Presidents & Athletic Directors

- Teachers and Educational Institutions

- Sport Organizations, Private Athletic Clubs, Leagues, Public Activity Centers

- Team managers, trainers, doctors, and support staff that watch and care for athletes

- Parents, family, and friends of beginner to elite athletes.

My intention is to lead you through this book and match your desire to be the best "You" you can be. What do you want to learn? And how do you want to impact your athlete's development? Inside these pages, I will take you on a deep-thinking journey. There are seven chapters, and each has a profound emphasis on the mental and emotional aspect to sports. Plus, the flow of information is organized to help readers grasp and immediately apply the knowledge in real world scenarios.

Chapter 1 is based on one of my most compelling inspirations for writing this book: identifying hurtful behavior and abuse. We must be familiar with certain words and behaviors and able to identify abuse in order to protect our athletes and create real change. Chapter 2 moves into understanding the practices of "higher-mind" thinking, transcending challenges with the Underdog Mentality, and being deliberate in guiding young people in sports. Chapter 3 explores the complex human being, perceiving each athlete as whole and unique, and how to use that to develop a meaningful human connection. Chapter 4 embraces *Partnerships*—a fresh and innovative model of coaching and teaching. Learn to create a "power balance" and a fabulous working relationship that empowers athletes to speak up and be brave, which triggers more motivation and success! Chapter 5 walks you through the awareness needed to gain clarity in recognizing common negative habits in sports. "The ruler" is the opposite of being a "partner" with athletes. The ruler over-powers and causes doubt, confusion, and anxiety. Be aware of various negative habits! Chapter 6 soars with the Psychology of Learning, providing positive communication and actual teaching methods that are effective and transformative for coaches and parents while guiding and elevating athletes and their confidence. Finally, Chapter 7 is about believing that anything is possible! Mental training techniques are the groundwork in how to manage thoughts and feelings. Teach athletes to identify fears, develop the skill of believing, and integrate mental training into practice time to enhance self-awareness and safety in the sports environment. Awesome!

This book is not meant to be swallowed up in one or two readings. This is an ongoing friend and mentor for you. Take your time in any of the sections that resonate with you. Go back and re-read to practice and apply new thoughts. Talk about what you're learning. From beginning to end, you'll gain insight from influencers in philosophy and positive psychology; innovative teachings from sports legends and leaders in education. You get to *expand your perception* on fundamental human behavior. You also get to practice the humanistic approach, including empathy and its amazing power. Your communication skills will grow. And you'll be able to learn basic mental training and emotional intelligence to go inward and acquire the wise balance needed in sports. With this book, you can enhance your awareness of conscious thought through "slowing down." Use mindfulness, feel the waves of clarity in the calm. You can achieve that feeling, regularly.

Focused and Inspired can reconnect everyone in the sports community, and as human beings, renewing ourselves with respect for the learning process. You will discover, or *rediscover*, the brightest part of yourself and the greatest capacity to guide athletes with your whole heart and mind.

Thank you for reading this book. Thank you for advocating for change. Thank you for helping young athletes learn how to be mentally and emotionally aware and know that their voices matter. Because when an athlete experiences respect and balanced power with their coach or any adult, it becomes a dynamic partnership that will produce confidence and wholeness. Together, we will manifest a new culture and keep our athletes safe.

CHAPTER 1

I'll Protect Every One of You!

*Safety is a feeling. Beyond rules and policies,
the athletes' emotions are the voices to follow.*

L isten. Listen to athletes. Listen with deep compassion so they will feel a close connection. Athletes will then experience more confidence, they'll know the peace and surety of safety, and your attention and care will prevent abuse and relieve any suffering. To keep athletes safe and help them thrive are both wise and ethical. In that, we must become highly aware of the signs of negative behavior and the root problems of abuse. Moreover, we can practice the positive ways to speak, motivate, and guide athletes. These methods are not intuitive or learned overnight, and they are not learned in a safety code of rules. Understanding the mental and emotional scope in sports is a journey in itself. Continual reading and sharing will forge feelings of calm and the habit of observing yourself and others. You'll be more attentive to words and messages; you'll implement new tactics and do everything you can to facilitate safe environments, relationships, and protect our athletes. Pressing forward with the spirit of change—together, we can do this!

The Sports World is Waking up

In 2017, we became acutely aware of the win-at-all-costs culture we've created, and the painful and serious affect it has had on our

athletes. Instead of developing self-assured, happy people, we've asserted *our power* and put prestige, egos, and gold medals, first. This problem became dreadfully apparent with over three hundred female athletes reporting horrific ongoing sexual abuse by the same doctor in the sports environment. It spanned over twenty years and we were shocked. Pointedly, it was the lack of attention, safety, autonomy, and respect for young athletes.

Verbal and emotional abuse laid a foundation of fear and allowed the sexual abuse to happen over and over. These girls could not talk, no one would listen. They were trapped, and their voices didn't matter.

In a courtroom in January 2018, one hundred and fifty-six brave women gave victim impact-statements that revealed a long-standing culture of fear and terrible control. In a "power-over" mindset and state of command, coaches and administrators had governed and made rules so that no one would question them. This misuse of power caused mass confusion, fear, doubt, and extreme limitation of anyone's ability to speak up, especially the athletes.

Facts: control manipulates; anger manipulates. There are thousands of wonderful coaches and supporters in sports, but control is very present. It is widespread and prevalent at the top, in the middle, and at every level. Control is pushed into the athlete's mind, into the attitude and spirit so far that *they* don't even realize what's happening. They are pushed into vulnerable submission because "that's what it takes" to be good. When coaches insist on having complete authority over every aspect of training, there's a problem. When decisions are made only by the coach, and athletes start to feel unsafe, that is wrong. When sharp words and actions diminish an athlete's vitality, and parents are unaware and unable to help, it is extremely damaging.

There is reason to pause and reflect, because it's both logical and crucial to *rethink how we motivate*. Our tone, what we say, and what we do has lasting impact. We've heard the voices. The worst abuse case *ever* in the history of sports is waking us up. We are now listening to athletes; we're learning to change our coaching behavior, our group behavior; and we are creating a new culture of education, safety, positive interactions, and training standards. As a broader sports community, including sports administrators, staff, and parents, too, we submitted to "authorities" and went along with dysfunctional leadership for one-dimensional success. No longer. It's time to change. We hear the athletes and we will rise. We have been influenced and suckered into an epidemic of results and selfishness. Again, no longer. It's time to change. We all hear the athletes and *we will rise.*

- Now, instead of win at all cost, we will put care above all.

- Now, instead of closed doors and one mind, we will advocate for transparency and many minds.

- Now, instead of hurry-up-and-win, we will sloooww down and teach.

It's time…it's time to follow the wisdom of intangible values and make our young athletes' health and well-being the top priority. I invite you to read thoroughly and think deeply about becoming more aware. Let's talk about abuse and how to keep athletes safe.

Verbal and Emotional Abuse

Zero. Our mission is Zero Tolerance for verbal and emotional abuse. First, you need to be aware and recognize the signs. As you read and grasp the symptoms and behaviors of verbal and emotional abuse, talk to athletes. Teach them the signs in a kind and thoughtful manner. Be open and listen to what they say. This may not be simple, but it is *crucial* that we create a dialogue and learn from each other.

- It can be hard to detect verbal and emotional abuse because words do not leave evidence, except what you feel inside *after* you've been abused.

- There is great confusion, sadness, loneliness, and emotional scars.

- For athletes, "confusion" is a terrible part of being abused because the abuser appears to be a "normal" person in public, but in private, they become very different.

- Look out because one minute the abuser is nice, the next they are angry.

- One second the abuser gives a compliment and the next, they criticize, belittle, and yell.

- In closed practices or off to the side of a gym, field, or game, the abuser uses different emotions and tactics to control an athlete.

- Abusers are secretive and may threaten athletes not to tell anyone what they said or did.

Types of Abuse & Common Tactics to Manipulate and Control Athletes:

Rude or mean behavior	"You'll never move up. You don't have the talent."
Ordering	"Stop walking. No, don't get a drink. Get back over here."
Name calling	"You're nothing. Only stupid people do that."
Bullying	"Ohh, you're tired? Does the baby need a nap?"
Threatening	"Run that slow again, you'll keep running till you cry."
Intimidation	(standing super close) "You better make the next goal."

Dismisses pain or discomfort	"You're not hurt. Tell me the bone is sticking out."
Blaming and Criticizing	"You're always screwing it up for the team. You don't care."
Denial and Lying	"I never said that! You're making it all up."
Pressure	"Do that skill now or forget."
Anger	"I'm sick and tired of you not listening!"

"Anger abuse" is very common and, usually, the abuser carries inner tension. He/she may laugh about something, then turn on a dime and scream at an athlete, like a bully, scaring the team, too. Then they act like it's all your fault. They call you names, like "Brainless." Everyone, even parents, tolerate it, yet feel like they have to be careful and "walk on egg shells." *Don't make the abuser mad. Don't get on his/her bad side.*

Recognize More Signs that Athlete-Victims Experience

When an athlete is frequently nervous because they might upset the coach, and they pay close attention, stiff with worry, that's a glaring sign of intimidation and fear. When an athlete starts to defend a mean coach, they may actually be protecting themselves. When athletes feel like they are one person (quiet and nervous) around the coach, and a totally different person (relaxed and happy) away from the coach— it's not the sport that worries them, it's the coach—and that's not a healthy dynamic. Especially when the athlete is expending more than half of their thoughts and energy to *not upset the coach*. It's true and this is so common that many athletes get used to the habit of flashing their attention back and forth, from their activity to their coach, to make absolutely sure the coach is pleased. They do not sustain focus. It becomes clear after a while, that the athlete is not fully concentrating on their skills—*because they are worried about the coach's reaction.*

Frequent verbal and emotional abuse has created panic, depression, vulnerability, and great fear in young athletes, so they **cannot** stop it. Sarcastic and callous language, hostile body language, and rigid, uncompromising rules from a coach or adult causes pain.

Almost always, abuse comes from a person who is older, bigger, smarter, and has a dominant position. They have the power.

It's extremely difficult for athletes to identify, speak up, and manage abuse, because they are

- smaller

- younger

- not as experienced

- not able to articulate their thoughts and feelings

- and people are very likely to believe the abuser when they explain their side.

If there is one incident with an adult abusing an athlete, the adult should be dealt with immediately and swiftly. Do not wait. Do not give second chances. Protect the athletes.

Grooming

Grooming is the process and strategic actions of a predator who is preparing their victim to be most vulnerable and abuse them in secret.

When athletes are mistreated in sports, they become vulnerable. The more vulnerable, worried, and scared athletes feel, the more likely they are to be targeted for sexual abuse. Young people who have more free time, they're parents are gone a lot, or they aren't supervised by someone who is safe and trustworthy—those young people will be targeted by a predator.

The person doing the grooming is often very complimentary; they try to get invited to events, stick around, and can give off an awkward energy at times. But they smile and "seem nice." A predator also gives gifts, just to be nice, or tells the athlete "they thought they could use" an item, so now they appear helpful. Predators are not one type of person: they are male and female; they are young and old, related to family or unrelated, closely involved with a team, or maybe a community member. You never know, so it's important to understand the outward signs and your internal feelings.

Overall, the more we talk to and listen to athletes, the more we describe feelings of being uncomfortable or confused, *then* we are informing athletes and keeping them close to us—and keeping them away from danger.

Teach athletes to notice signs of feeling uncomfortable, anxious, or fearful. See Chapter 7 about symptoms of fear. If there is any sign of a predator, or feeling scared of someone, that requires immediate attention. Do not linger for a week. If you are busy, athletes need to get help from another adult, coach, administrator, or parent—but attend to this right away. This is their life.

Learn Safety Basics

1. Safety in sports should be a normal topic to discuss. Just like hiking and staying on a marked trail, we also keep our minds and bodies safe on a "positive trail" with people, every day. There's a lot to enjoy, but look out for the dangers.

2. Keep discussions with athletes age appropriate—children up to fifth grade do not learn about mature topics in school, like abuse or sex education, so keep it simple for young athletes. Even for mid-

dle graders and teens, we don't want to scare them or worry them, because that makes them more fearful and vulnerable. Ask them questions like, "What safety measures do you follow at home? or What have you learned about safety?" That may open up the conversation, or at least it lets them know you are curious and they can talk to you later.

3. Use calm voices and propose reasonable steps to stay safe. Keep the language positive and always give options for getting help; names, phone numbers, and other resources. This is wise and responsible conversation and athletes will feel grateful.

4. Post Signs and Policies, talk and brag about safety discussions, keep the conversation going.

5. Young people should never, never be alone with an adult who is not family. Doors and window covers are *always* open. *Never* be alone for a private lesson, driving, traveling, medical appointments, trying on clothes, meetings, or a personal issue. Always have a third person there.

Safety should be a regular topic with your sports program and in your family. It's great to be safe! Have the athletes make a "Safety Poster" or plan a "Safety Party" with yummy food, games, and music. Celebrate that safety is a wonderful activity and precaution—we take care of ourselves and each other. And a terrific part is education and learning about emotions. Emotions are the first signal to becoming alert.

Emotions are warnings for athletes, and they need to be in tune to recognize the warnings.

Practical Tips — How to facilitate Emotional Intelligence (EQ)

Emotional intelligence, or EQ, is recognizing emotions in yourself, understanding *why* you're having certain feelings, and *managing* your emotions in a mature and thoughtful manner. (In Chapter 2, read more details about inner awareness.) Now, to help athletes manage their emotions, you will look at yourself. You will pay attention to your patterns of thought, speech, and choices. For instance, do you usually enter practice thinking, *I want the team to make progress today!* If so, how does that feel to you? Exciting? Worrisome? Stressful? We cannot teach, unless we truly understand and practice attention on our own thoughts and feelings.

Practical Tips — How to Teach EQ

1. Make one week: "I will pay attention to my thoughts and feelings." Keep a small notebook with you and take notes.

2. Tell your athletes, "I'm paying attention to my thoughts and feelings this week!" Smile big, show them your notebook, tell them you're learning about yourself to be a better coach! This will be curious to them, and gently suggest they might do it, too… (depending on age and desire. Do not have expectations. You are leading by example.)

3. Buy and put up a "Chart of Emotions" or "Feelings Chart" with faces and feelings. Put this chart on a wall or bring it to practices for discussion. Point to the faces and ask if they've had that feeling before and to describe what happened. Just listen and observe. Be supportive in whatever they experienced. This is wonderful conversation!

4. Explain to your athletes that you value everyone's feelings, you believe in good communication, knowing how they feel, and being able to help them in practice.

Emotions Chart

CONFIDENT

RELIEVED

CONFUSED

CALM

WORRIED

SCARED

5. For one month, be intentional and use the Emotions Chart for conversation about yourself; how you enter practice, plan group and individual assignments, prepare them for move-up skills, testing, and meets. Maybe document how you felt when something happened in your life.

Talking about emotions brings your athletes' attention to what they feel and think. In a team talk, maybe sitting in a circle, tell your athletes you respect their thoughts and feelings. Then...*ask!* Ask them what they think and feel about sports. Ask them, "How do you feel today? How do you feel about doing challenging moves or plays?" Point to the face "Relieved" and ask when they remember feeling relieved about something: what was that like? And, maybe when they felt "Excited." Start with the light-hearted emotions (not betrayed or insecure). Get to heavier emotions another day after a group conversation and giggles.

Focus on the process and not certain answers. Everything is good. All answers are acceptable, as long as they are respectful and kind. Honor everyone's feelings. Make sure to say, "Thank you for being so honest. You are brave to share your feelings. Really." In sports, or at home, these are simple, practical ways to teach emotional intelligence and awesome team and family support. You can do it!

How to Talk about Sensitive Issues

Talking to young people about sensitive issues requires care. You might be nervous. They might be nervous. They'll wonder if we can be patient, see it from their view, and believe them. An athlete's highest desire is that you will listen to them...and care. Both of you can take a deep breath and promise to be patient, kind, and respectful. In one-on-one conversations, remember to keep doors and windows open and always have a third person present or nearby where they can see you. Now...take a deep breath and believe in the safety you are teaching...

Listen to Athletes

1. Before you start a sensitive conversation, get into a mindful place in your heart and mind, and connect to your own intention of practicing empathy toward your athlete.

2. Do not rush, do not get distracted, and please do not dismiss their thoughts or feelings. Focus on this important young person and the process of listening and practicing safety.

3. Smile, take a breath, and notice their eyes, their body language, their voice, and how much of a struggle or pain they're feeling. Pause...be very present with them.

4. Tell them things like this:

   I'm really glad to speak with you and help you.

   I'm open to whatever is on your mind or bothering you.

   Sports can be really challenging, so it's good for us to talk.

   I will listen, and you can ask me any questions you like.

   We will find ways to make things better.

   I appreciate your privacy, and we will figure this out together.

They may not tell you everything, but they know you are a safe place to go. And together you can figure it out. If you see or hear signs of danger (with an adult or anyone), if you're worried about the safety of the athlete and/or other athletes, consider reporting it to local officials. When you hear clear evidence that abuse is going on, or the athlete is definitely at risk, report the abuser to the police, immediately, and include the NGB, National Governing Body, of your sport. Take the steps. Do not let someone talk you out of it or give the abuser another chance. We must protect every athlete and young person.

Teammate Bullying

Is bullying happening on your team? Or, is there bullying in your family? You may not realize it, but it happens. Young people pick on each other, and no one stops it. At home, parents are distracted and busy. In sports, athletes get depressed, scared, and freak out in practice or a game. An athlete is targeted and bullied, but he/she will not speak up more than once to coaches or parents. If that. Because they are afraid of retaliation and scared that it may get worse.

Recognize common problems, because some adults…

- do not believe young people when they speak up

- brush it aside because "that's just how they are"

- don't prioritize respect and use positive words, so it never gets handled properly. Then it is ignored.

I believe we coach and support athletes because we care about them. But many times, we are task-oriented (clean up your room, do your homework, take out the trash), or we get swallowed up in coaching technique and skills, only. We get distracted and *do not attend* to shaping young people with *character*. Let's shift our thinking and behaviors, and model the highest integrity to keep athletes safe.

Suggestions to Reinforce Respect & Safety with Teammates:

1. Teach, share, and follow a Safety Code for your sport to the letter, talk about it, refer to it, and promote respect, kindness, and cooperation.

2. Sit your team down for an hour or more. Talk it all out. Do not practice. *Talk and listen.* Lay down specific values and moral character as the highest priority. (See "Your Values" section in Chapter 3.)

3. If you need a guide or facilitator, find one. A counselor, sport psychologist, or mental training coach can help with the ease and formalities so that the tone is comfortable yet memorable.

4. Do an activity every week for 5-minutes. Create fun ways to be kind, patient, and boost each other up. For instance, when an athlete says to their teammate, "How can I support you?" that is positive and helpful. Athlete safety happens through connection and kind words!

Under the Surface, Body Language Speaks Loudly

Look at your athletes—how they stand, sit, listen, and talk. Is their chin up? Is their mouth tight? What does their body say? Do they lean in to talk, or do they keep a distance? Are their eyes glazed-over in practice, or do they avoid looking at you?

When athletes don't speak, they are still telling you something. Body language is a tool for us to learn and connect with our athletes. Face and body-language *is* a language.

I'm great friends with an Olympic water polo coach who truly enjoys getting to know his athletes. He asks questions. He jokes around, finds out what they want and need, and "how they tick."

When coaches truly care, when they communicate well and partner with athletes, they keep athletes safe. When we want athletes to open up to us, we can create a safe and trusting space to do so **with our attention.**

Look *under* the surface. Look at the way they hold their hands together, tightly in front of them, or how they look down at the ground, as if they are sad or lonely, or what about the way they shift their weight from right to left. Do they have nervous energy? Are they intimidated by all the talent around them? Maybe they are anxious in a positive way—to get out on the field and prove to you that they are determined and good! Be aware, your presence is "authority" and athletes struggle to speak up. They do. So, be that positive partner: Get down on your knee, smile, look into their eyes and for 10-seconds, take a breath with your athlete, stay right there and ask, "How do you feel?" or "What do you think?" If they pause, offer options. "Are you nervous?" "Worried?" "Unsure if you can do the skill?"

Athletes might open up, might, but the biggest success here is that they know you care. You are creating a safe place for them to seek help. With your kind patience and attention, you've set the precedence to talk about feelings. For the thousands of athletes who've been mistreated and abused, you are creating change in how we treat them. You are engaging in important human relations, showing you care, and demonstrating moral and ethical behavior.

Ethics in Sports is the Beginning of Safety

Summarizing this chapter on protecting athletes, we are reminded that teaching and coaching athletes requires good morals and ethical behavior. As a coach, parent, and supporter of athletes, *we are all engaging in moral work.* We don't discuss this much, but ethics in sports is foundational, it's the study and application of moral principals, including autonomy, that guide our behavior with athletes. Please consider: How are you guiding your athletes, and on what do you base your behavior? Have you considered that coaching is an inherently ethical enterprise? It really is. It's wonderful and important for all of us to take a pause and think deeply about how we affect young people in sports. Instead of being re-active, let's be pro-active. My suggestion is to start with the real intention to go "outside the box" and stretch into the human side of sport, not just the technical. Look closely at your interpersonal interactions with athletes. Examine the moral dimensions of your aim in coaching. With your choice to listen to athletes, you are showing them that their thoughts, feelings, and safety matter more than winning, more than anything else in the whole wide world. Let's keep reading and practice *listening*.

CHAPTER 2

I Hear You!

We are all the creators of human nature:
your choices do make a difference.

Dream Big

Kids. Kids are cute, bouncy, and eager, and they are a blast to coach. The most wonderful part is talking to athletes about their goals and helping them reach their dreams. I've been touring for many months, sharing my books and mental training program. When kids meet me, their eyes smile. They tell me their names and I teach them about the power of their thoughts and how to use mental skills. I call it "mental powers!" And do you know what? They become fascinated! Teenagers appear mesmerized and grin. Younger kids shout, "I'm terrific!" and say over and over, "I am strong! I am strong! I am strong!" Before my very eyes, I see how daring they are to learn things they've never tried. I feel their desire to discover their abilities and picture their dreams. I hear their voices, talking with me and connecting, and I am honored. They open up and trust me. For a while, I get to be their partner in the learning process. I get to teach them and learn from them. Through sincerity and true emotion, the work feels promising, and dreams seem brighter.

These types of thoughts and feelings are not shallow—they go deep. When we generate a vibrant connection with athletes, a bond is formed. Then, we can go harder and tackle the significant work in sports. To do that, athletes need to know they have reliable support.

Parents and coaches, your frequent interaction has significant impact on your athletes. How you talk and listen to each other creates a synergetic support that bolsters confidence. Consider the strength of *your* thoughts. In order to raise the bar in your athlete's performance, consider *your* emotions. When you get in tune with yourself, your calm voice, and your positive desires, you are much more compelling. When done intentionally, you are using higher-mind thinking.

Higher-Mind Thinking

To attain a level of excellence in sports, the process demands incredible commitment. It also requires a coach's technical vigilance and reflection on the *human calculation*. Human calculation in sport is applying an introspective view of the athletes' ability to perform, but only after time observing, and observing closely, and asking yourself important questions, like:

- How hard can I push them?
- Is fifteen more minutes of conditioning likely to build their strength or give them doubts?
- Do they need a mental rest, maybe a light day, to come back more motivated?
- That athlete is starting to slow down, is he losing confidence?

The greatest coaches and leaders are deliberate. They take time and prepare their minds—for the goals they've set, and what they are about to do. They deeply consider their words, tone, and the impact they want to make.

When you are intentional with your thoughts and feelings, daily, and consider how you impact others, you are aware. You are developing and using higher-mind thinking.

This book is intended to enhance your life and improve the working relationship and outcomes with your athletes by sharpening your higher-mind thinking. As you watch, listen, and connect with athletes in more meaningful ways, consider *new perspectives* in the human calculation. A change in approach occurs best through higher-mind thinking. So, pause and think, *what is your desire? And, what is your athlete's desire?* Take some time. Examine your thoughts and words and create strong, positive patterns of new thoughts.

Exercise: New Thinking
Check off these list-items as you do them and practice using them.

Think about a recent time your athlete seemed tired or lacked motivation. What were you thinking or feeling? Did you get impatient, or did you manage the situation positively? What did you say? Was there tension? If you had the chance, would you change anything? Describe your thoughts then, and how you might respond, now:

_____

_____

_____

At practices, watch your emotions closely around your athletes. This is not natural when you are typically analyzing *their effort*. Now, notice how *you feel* and own it. Notice the beginning of disappointment or frustration, then pause and understand this is your feeling. You can change it if you want. Write down what has triggered your feelings in the recent past, so you can become aware. Describe here:

_____

_____

_____

Practice pausing, take a breath, reflect on the athletes and what's most important for them to be in a positive mindset. Take another breath and exhale all the way out. Make a commitment to being calm while considering the athlete's goals and respecting the athlete's feelings. Write a few words of this commitment:

_____

_____

_____

Think about the message you want to give each athlete. Think about how your words will affect them. Ponder personalities, recent training, if they're struggling or doing well. Write down some phrases you'd like to say to two or three athletes:

_____

_____

_____

Talk to athletes, thoughtfully, compliment them, get to know them, form a bond. Write down true positive statements about your athletes, and the goals they want to reach:

_____

_____

_____

The relationship and training dynamic begin to change as we get in tune. As you practice positive perspectives, as you apply new intentions, you will look more deeply into each athlete as a complex person with thoughts and feelings. They will guide you in *how to support them.* Slow down, think about your feelings, and increase your emotional awareness.

It's more common for us to *not contemplate* or be deliberate. Most people, who are on task, react to situations and do not plan ahead. Most coaches focus on instructions and results, parents have to-do lists, and it ends up we don't spend time thinking about how we impact our athletes. Let's practice more awareness.

But first, I have a confession. I was not good at this in my early years of coaching. My need to work hard and mold tough athletes was extreme. I was determined to make them good! (Because I was a tough athlete and that strict style was what I learned.) I was fully in tune with my desire. I ended up getting feedback on my approach: "Lisa, you're too hard on the kids. Ease up a bit." I didn't want to hear that. *What!?* I was conflicted, but it made me stop and think. I noticed I felt tense in practices. Did my expectations fit the athletes? Was I consumed with my past training methods, or was I bringing something new and growing the sport? If I was "too hard," was my coaching approach the best way?

Self-awareness and emotional awareness develop a deeper intelligence to coach more effectively. When you are emotionally aware, you'll notice sooner when you start to feel things, like disappointment or frustration. You'll see challenges rise...and manage them with a calmer mind.

If athletes are dodging "verbal bullets" and tension from a coach, then they are not focused on their work. They are distracted and concerned with pleasing you. But your self-awareness will inspire mindful and productive practices for your team. From an empathic connection with athletes, being patient and positive, they will trust you and gain insight into how they can also be in tune and in control of themselves. There are so many distractions in sports, but by focusing attention *inward*, you and your athletes will find it is quite different and surprisingly nice!

Go Inward

Focus on inner experiences. Go inward and you will be able to un-derstand yourself and your athletes better. You will nurture a safe, confident feeling in them while being highly productive.

Emotional awareness is the ability to identify feelings; this is a foundation for emotional intelligence.

Emotional intelligence is understanding a) why you're having certain feelings, and b) managing your emotions in a mature and thoughtful manner.

Self-awareness is the ability to a) know what you're doing as you do it, and b) understand why you're doing it.

Empathy is recognizing, caring for, and acknowledging the feel-ings of others.

As you and your athletes become aware of thoughts and feelings, criti-cal or kind, positive or negative, you will both develop the *ability to choose*. Choose your thoughts. Choose your feelings. I ask athletes, "What do you want?" As they hear that question, they get to think and decide. Instead of feeling confused and out of control, they are be-ing still, thoughtful, and processing their desires. I encourage them, I say, "You choose. You decide. YOU are powerful!" And then, they feel it…this incredible connection of higher-mind thinking, because they are in control, they are connected to their desire, and we are focused and inspired *together*.

Feeling Powerful is Everything

Every child struggles with something. No one is immune. And especially in sports, they want to *feel* powerful. They want to "live high" and reach their dreams. For coaches and parents, it's the most important part of our job to build their self-esteem and lift them up, because the journey is rough. Rarely is a kid the "favorite," or the popular one. Most athletes—in grade school, high school, even college—they are continually striving, climbing, trying to keep up. They are the *underdog*. Being an underdog is totally normal, but athletes don't like struggling. No one does, right? So, when they experience a synergy of convincing support—from coaches, parents, and teammates—and when they practice mental and emotional training, they can focus on all of that conviction and feel more confident inside. They grow mental powers to be clear, strong, and focused while preparing for competition. Maybe they *will* reach their dreams!

Because when athletes feel in control and in charge of themselves, they are not just the underdog striving, they start to become...heroes.

The Underdog Mentality

As you know, the *favorite* team in a sports game typically has a history of winning, awesome talent, evidence of skill and winning momentum, the reputation of greatness, often the officials' partiality, and rich excitement from the fans, which helps in conquering opponents.

On the other hand, there is the *underdog*. Do athletes want to be the underdog? No, not usually. But, when athletes connect with the Underdog Mentality and their true inner strength, they find there's an all-powerful feeling inside them and they become *heroic*. Let's learn...It is heroic for athletes to think, act, and speak from their greatest desire, all the while clear that they are the underdog. It is heroic to go after what they want with astounding dedication, knowing the climb ahead is steep, rough, and scary, unsure of how far they'll go. It is heroic to be brave in the face of pressure, to grab onto the hardest fight and rise in spirit to perform their best. It is heroic to risk those moments of danger; danger of not performing well and "losing face" if one fails. And one of the greatest heroic moments is bowing low and graciously after the fight, win or lose, and genuinely saying, "Thank you. Thank you for the opportunity. I am so humbled and grateful to be here."

It takes real intention to model this attitude. It takes true purpose to speak each day from this mindset of humility and magnificent desire. You have such influence with your athletes. Treasure that and dance in it because your intentions and purpose can produce magic, and *that* inspires greatness. At the 2018 NCAA National Championships in women's gymnastics, the country witnessed stunning heroics. Six teams in the finals, the competition was intense and had incredible talent. High performances on every turn. In the last two events, UCLA was lagging, Oklahoma was winning, and several other teams were in the hunt. When you looked at the scoreboard, it was obvious Oklahoma had it in the bag…UCLA didn't think they could win. But suddenly, they decided to fight anyway. Instead of having to be "the top dog" in the standings, they decided to win their own hearts. Instead of having to be perfect under pressure, they chose to simply *feel joy*—in the moment—with their audience. They leapt into "delight" and embodied the essence of happiness. While Oklahoma was moments away from capping off a third consecutive national title, UCLA did it. They played like children. They were fearless. On the last event, beam (often said to be the most difficult event), each team member hit like it was a picnic in the park. They flipped across the beam, invincible! And the final performer pranced and danced to score the ultimate 10.0. The team's beam score ended up as the highest in NCAA history. And UCLA edged out the Sooners to win the National Championship!

I get goosebumps thinking about it. It was captivating. To see those women exude that brilliant attitude in the sports world at this time, under incredible pressure—wow! It was exactly what we needed. With the past culture (and brainwashing in sports believing that ruthless hard work and seriousness are the only path to winning medals), we are in desperate need of reminders of a better and healthier way. The power of each athlete's personal desire was evident with the UCLA gymnastics team. We see again that "the possible"—coming from behind to win an NCAA National title—happens when we come together with the most profound human spirit.

When we believe and trust...magic can happen.

Transcend Challenges

The high road inspires us. It creates a spark inside athletes to shine their brightest, feel safe, and perform their best. When we encourage athletes and view them as significant and valuable, we are on that road. Paved with kindness, patience, and joy, this road connects people. The Underdog Mentality is based in humility and human connection, it is *not* focused on results. And through this mentality, athletes transcend physical challenges. They surpass the obstacles of soreness and pain, they embrace hard work with a joyful attitude. The Underdog Mentality is the antidote for doubt. It is the remedy for "less than" or "small." And to be honest, it conquers almost anything. Because underdogs grow to treasure the spirit of virtuous thought and action. When you focus on being happy while working hard, athletes get it, especially as they witness their progress. Graciousness trickles down from coaches to athletes. They become filled with gratitude.

We *teach the values* of the underdog mentality every day. The principal factor is modeling patience and positivity, which naturally influences athletes to chase their dreams. After a fall, they pick themselves up, they keep striving and have a much better chance at feeling confident. In the midst of a struggle, when we say, "You can do it! Try again! I know you can," with a smile and sureness, we literally influence athletes. And not just one day, but every day.

These attitudes can absolutely persuade, but it must be a pattern. Athletes need to feel they can rely on coaches and parents to consistently provide positive support and a safe bond. If you feel that scores and winning have been the focus, then change it. Because what's happening in our sports world is a detriment to each athlete's personal development. Inside, they don't feel good enough.

Our need to have success is a superficial design in our society, and we have designed it. *Individual choices matter, and your choices either continue group behavior, or change it.*

We have been drawn to value material rewards of glory, so we've pursued it, perpetuated it, and we have failed our children. Athlete health and well-being is the highest goal. *And we can still win!* By adopting this mindset of athlete wellness and the underdog mentality, you will likely win more. Feeling like a hero is pretty powerful stuff! It may take time, but we can detach from the "superficial" and realign with what's meaningful and inspiring. In order to shift, we need to practice *awareness*. We must become acutely aware of our thoughts and feelings. It is vital—if we want to transform.

You Gotta Go Deep

Let's go deep. In order to practice awareness and teach what's most important, coaches have to get to know themselves, deeply, as well. Are you with me? Because schedules often dictate, we all get tense and worried. *Oh shoot, we're late!* Not prepared, distracted, frustrated. Or we're preoccupied with bosses, staff, or parents. We are worried. Honestly, what is stressing us…*is us*. Athletes face *their* fears and manage anxieties to perform their best, and so we must face ours. But we stuff it down. We focus on the athlete. Our inner dialogue or subconscious says: "Don't think about it, just keep going." But you're likely teaching your athlete to ignore stress and not to talk about it—keep everything inside. Everyone is carrying tension.

If we want athletes to positively face their fears and manage their anxieties, then we must face ours with genuine interest and care. Take steps to talk! Be honest and respectful with yourself and others. Don't hold grudges or anger. Tension is not helpful. In sports, we fight to push through pressure and get past it, but it's there…it's always there unless you deal with it. If you are disconnected from root feelings, if you are ignoring what's most important, it's time to be brave, go deep, and work it out. Your personal inner process is a gift for you to transform. Start the process and take action.

Exercise: Let Go of Tension

Flesh out thoughts, feelings, and tension. Write some things on your mind that you've been holding in, or anything that is simply bothering you, and plan to talk it out.

1. _____

2. _____

3. Set a date and time to talk it out: _____

Letting go of problems and tension allows you to feel and be more peaceful. Then, you can reflect and switch to higher-mind thinking. Now, just like some of the great coaches in sport, and some of our inspired thinkers, you can practice authenticity and amazing human connection.

Wired for Human Connection

Phil Jackson, 11-Time NBA Champion Coach, has been called the Zen Coach: A deep-thinking and influential leader, he taught the power of ceremony and beliefs from Native Americans and Buddhists. He demonstrated to his team that following personal rituals of going inward and connecting to their peaceful center creates greater harmony—and physical flow. In his book *Sacred Hoops*, Phil tells stories about coaching the Chicago Bulls and teaching a spiritual, selfless mindset. Honor the self and honor others. That was foundational for the tough basketball players. They committed to non-violence and non-aggression on the court. Daily, they practiced being "awake," aware, and in tune. Mental training, or mindfulness, was different from anything they'd done before. They sat still and quiet and learned how to slow their minds and be calm. The Bulls won three World Championships employing that calm emotion. A 'Zen' and humanistic approach.

Bill Walsh was a legendary football coach. With the San Francisco 49ers in the nineteen-eighties, he won 3 NFL Super Bowl Championships. He was known for his creativity, innovation, and his skill of teaching—with *wisdom*. He was nicknamed "The Genius." Bill also coached the football team at Stanford University in the nineteen-nineties, while I was coaching the Stanford women's gymnastics team. In my role as head coach, I had taught the women how to slow down and connect with their inner quiet self, much like Phil Jackson's philosophy, incorporating rituals. I was young leading a Division I college program, and I had learned at Stanford many winning coaches in our athletic department spoke to teams in other sports— and they had remarkable influence. Upon my request, Bill Walsh came and spoke to my team; I was jumping out of my skin. He spoke to my athletes before a big competition, and what a great man, what a wise presence he was. First, he was tall and walked in with a smile and sureness, like he always knew where he was going. White wavy hair, and a purposeful, gentle voice, he exuded insight and sharp thoughts. We were quiet and listened closely. Bill described the incredible tension at football games. He said when they travelled to another stadium, the home crowd roared so loudly and made such a ruckus, that it literally disarmed other visiting teams. So, he instructed his players to huddle up, closely, and look into each other's eyes. They placed their hands on each other's shoulders, encouraged each other, and felt their unified energy. He said the crowd's noise was such a force, the Stanford team allowed it, and imagined that it pushed them closer together and used it to feel their collective inner power. As they moved in closely, they morphed into a mental and emotional "chain" of magnificent strength. That *human connection* between one hundred young men was more powerful than the hundred-thousand fans screaming for the home team. He called it "100 vs. 100,000." Like David vs. Goliath—the Stanford team utilized their inner emotion… and *won.*

My team took Bill's advice and they, too, went beyond the call of expectation. A few weeks later, my team placed 9th in the country; the first time ever in Stanford history. These lessons about human behavior blow me away.

Brene Brown, a researcher, professor, and NY Times best-selling author, says we are wired for human connection. She is a highly sought-after speaker. Her wise and comical TED talk on vulnerability went viral; thirty million people have watched it. Without a doubt, her messages on vulnerability precisely relate to athletes and coaches because we have the ability to connect with each other by sharing our feelings and not holding them in. Brene's messages relate to exactly what we do in athletics. Because athletes need our consistent support, our aim is to form a human connection, one that is caring, motivating, and begins with being completely authentic.

Authentic Commitment with Your Athletes

Practice saying these statements, below, as a regular practice and reinforcement of your commitment. Maybe it's a monthly staff mantra! Consider putting it on a wall in big letters where all can see and read. Align your intention, put it "out there," that you will meet your athletes, daily, as intelligent and brave individuals. Be authentic.

1. Human connection is why I'm here, to guide and motivate athletes. I am neurologically wired to live and thrive through thoughtful human connection; supporting my athletes in sport is a significant way I can do that and make a positive difference.

2. I am committed to openly communicate with my athletes; through an open-mind, I can expand my perception of the interactions and emotions that drive training to be fulfilling.

3. Sport is "messy." Many emotions are present throughout. When an athlete feels something, it's real. I will pause, ask questions, and decide the best way to help them.

4. I will recognize and demonstrate that each athlete has value and is worthy of my attention, patience, and guidance. Their goals and desires are important to me.

5. I trust the learning process and believe that athletes need to enjoy playing sports. Their safety and well-being are the highest priorities.

Awareness Leads to Connection

We all want our athletes to reach their dreams. Wherever you are: in your kitchen; at a field, in France, Brazil, New Zealand, or America, wherever you are in the world, pause for a moment... Look deeply into yourself and commit. Make a promise you'll be more aware of yourself. Promise you'll look deeply into your athlete's heart and connect. Together you will be more powerful. *Together, you just might create heroic moments and dreams come true!*

CHAPTER 3

You're a Complex Human!

Each athlete is a multiplex of personal thoughts, ideas, and emotions. Look closely and learn.

The Humanistic Approach

Extraordinary. You are extraordinary to be self-aware and use higher-mind thinking in sports. Because playing sports is intense, and when you tell an athlete to be fierce and faultless one second, and 'ohhmmm' the next, that can be confusing. This chapter continues to expand your "awareness" in order to understand the nuances in how to connect with your athletes. There are tools and methods to help you, and you'll be able to find the delicate balance of the physical, mental, and emotional in training, by learning how to integrate the humanistic approach.

The Humanistic Approach focuses on each athlete as a whole and complex person who has essential needs, including psychological *and* emotional *needs.*

The Benefits in using the Humanistic Approach

You will…

- Understand each athlete, their personal values, what's important to them in life

- Find out what they need from you to feel supported and optimistic

- Realize which positive tactics will motivate each individual the best

- Pinpoint their various abilities / desires to capitalize on how they'll contribute to the team

- Make a habit of using curiosity and wisdom to truly connect and make thoughtful decisions

- See athletes perform with more passion and push through challenges with a better attitude

For coaches and parents, let's break it down and translate simple ways to connect and inspire!

Essential Needs for Athletes

Every athlete in every sport has significant inner needs, especially in connecting with coaches and parents. In their training program day in and day out, we must speak to them and build them up! Their psychological and emotional needs will be met when you follow these tips:

1. **Person-centered** - every person is different, trust their experience and instincts; allow the athlete to take the lead sometimes and discover their own solutions.

2. **Effort and strengths** - put attention on the effort (not results) and salute and celebrate personal assets as positives in the training process.

3. **Athlete's thoughts and feelings** - ask about their thoughts and feelings, acknowledge them, and listen. Do they feel safe? Do they feel useful and included? These are important.

4. **Open communication** - empower athletes to be leaders, speak honestly, even when it's uncomfortable. They need to feel valued and that you will respect them and work with them.

5. **Strategize together** - talk together, keep adjusting and find new approaches and ways to achieve goals. As they see their progress, their confidence builds.

I'll remind you of these essential needs throughout this book. And keep in mind, you are preparing your athletes not only for success in sports, but success in life. College applications, resumes, and interviews require our young people to *know* their strengths, *know* they can articulate their thoughts and feelings in a humble and truthful manner, *know* they can contribute their skills and keep growing. With patience and mindful support, coaches and parents show they care about the athlete as a person, rather than just as an athlete. Through the humanistic approach, athletes are more apt to tackle difficult challenges and commit to training standards. Listening to athletes is key. Listen to every voice, seek deeper understanding, and you will be on that high road creating an important human connection.

Apply These 'Humanistic' Examples in Practices

Notice how you can easily and consistently validate the athlete's feelings and intelligence and continue to engage them and inspire hard work.

- *Hey, everyone. Today, we'll talk for ten minutes. I'd like to hear your thoughts on our last competition.* *Coach wants to know about each athlete's thoughts and experience

- *You put a lot of focus into that drill. Great effort. On that throw, you made a quick read on the other players. Excellent decision.* *Coach identifies the athlete's effort, and strength in decision-making ability.

- *Okay, you said you're frustrated, and you don't feel your leg bending. Let's do a drill to practice squeezing your muscles and feeling a* *straight leg.* *Coach mirrors the athlete's words and addresses how to help fix the problem. Then they work together.

- *Coach, my run needs to get faster. Can you watch me next time and tell me what to focus on?* *The coach has set a tone and policy for open communication, so the athlete is not shy or worried, but can ask for specific assistance. This is training momentum.

- *You looked tense before your turn. What thoughts are you having? Maybe we can shift to a better mindset.* *Coach asks for feedback so the athlete can pause, rethink, then work together to create the best performance.

Exercise: Write Humanistic Phrases to Your Athletes

Think of one or two of your athletes. Write a phrase, how you can acknowledge their effort or a strength they have. This is important. For this exercise, leave out humor. Be sincere.

_____

_____

_____

Now, write a question to your athlete, a simple one to check in with how they're feeling. Then mirror, or repeat back, what you imagine them saying to you. Be positive and encouraging. End with a connection like, *I will help you*, or, *We can do this together.*

_____

_____

_____

Prepare to Coach and Guide the Whole Person

When you view the athlete as fabulous, complex, and intelligent, you'll see that kids are whole people! Not just athletes. They have family, friends, hobbies, dreams. For instance, does an athlete have four brothers and two sisters, or a dog named Charlie? Does their dad speak six languages? What books do 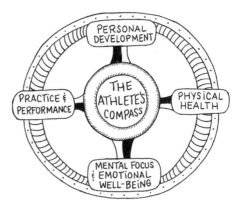 they like? Maybe they love nature hikes! By learning about athletes outside of the sport, you will gain insight to their personality, values, how to talk, help, and motivate the athlete as a "person."

1. Lead each practice with positive intentions and attitudes. As the coach, you get to set the tone! Let the athletes know you encourage open communication, that you are excited to be there, and you are passionate in developing each of them, especially when they need help or they're struggling.

2. *Before* you address an athlete, ask yourself first: Is it <u>true</u>, is it <u>kind</u>, is it <u>necessary</u>? If an athlete lacks talent for a skill or to advance to the next level, do not dash their dreams, but speak with open, honest communication and find a solution *that still inspires.*

3. Get in tune with empathy as your guide. An athlete's feelings, their fears and anxieties, are important. Acknowledge and be patient and you will win them over.

4. Listen actively. Focus your mind and heart 100% on the athlete you are listening to.

5. Non-judgmental caring. No judgment, no one is wrong. Everyone is in process.

6. Pay particular attention to the athlete's needs. Show you care about

the athlete's well-being and take steps to help them, instead of focusing on results.

Search online and watch the "Empathy" animated video, with Brene Brown as the narrator. This is an excellent teaching tool for coaches, parents, and supporters. I often show this video at coaching clinics and parent seminars. We are reminded to not dismiss an athlete's worries and don't try to fix it for them. Instead, be empathic. The video elicits a response that is not only positive, but in my clinics, coaches and parents smile, nod, and pause in reflection and mental lightbulbs start flashing. Wonderful conversation follows!

As you listen to and connect with your athletes, you will be enthralled with ways to propel their confidence. On that note, "Hurray for Positive Psychology!"

Positive Psychology inspires happiness, mental health, and drives a person through their strengths and abilities. It adds a richness in sports that points to the exact desire of all people — that we must **enjoy the process.**

We *get to be* positive, excited, and have fun! Coaching and parenting with Positive Psychology gives us the tools to engage athletes as people with thoughts and feelings. We identify their positive attributes and confirm the journey in attaining their goals. If you want to heighten your impact in coaching, parenting, or leadership, consider the following approach of a coach in Nevada, how she shapes the mood and environment in their gym. She responds in a relaxed and comical way, totally respecting the process, so her athletes can fail...and succeed.

A Coaching Evolution

Recently, I heard about a few Snapchat videos and I was intrigued, especially finding out the posts were from a top U.S. coach in Nevada.

I was traveling and visiting a gymnastics club in Utah, and the two coaches and myself were cracking up about this Nevada team and how their Snapchat videos are hilarious: the gymnasts take a turn on a skill, miss it, blow it, and the coach sort of shrugs and matter-of-factly says, "...okay." The athletes begin to giggle. It's nooo big deal. A mistake? "Okay." The Utah coaches loved it and said the videos have truly impacted their approach.

They still work hard and have strict standards, yet they've removed negative reactions and emotion. And their athletes do better.

What created this approach? The Nevada coach has always cared for the athlete as a person, first, but a big change was the fact she not only trained a group of gymnasts, but for a number of years, two of them were her teenage daughters. Daily, this top coach had to motivate her own daughters, without being too serious or too hard on them, or she would lose their motivation. To connect in an authentic way and get a good performance, she used the humanistic approach by observing, listening, and considering their thoughts and feelings. This style has been extremely successful for them. The athletes love their team and coaches, and training is challenging, productive, and meaningful—because they feel cared for.

We need to connect with athletes. When you only give orders, ignore athletes and disconnect from them, you will often provoke eye-rolls, refusal, or frustration. We are the adults, and we set the tone. It became crystal clear to the Nevada coach that the emotional factor was vital, and that all athletes needed more humor, patience, and respect. This situation impressed upon her to be *more mindful* in her coaching, relax more, add a little comedy, and draw them in. Drawww them in. This has produced a great working relationship with respect and incredible results.

The truth is athletes are already self-critical. When I trained and competed, I was incredibly hard on myself, a perfectionist; plus, I had strict coaches. I learned a lot, but the messages in my head were *no mistakes, not good enough,* and *be perfect, now.* Then I started coaching. I was wayyy too serious and impatient. I wanted results immediately. Thirty years later, I have more perspective than I did when I was in my twenties. I am a partner. I do not use negative emotions and I believe that humor is essential. I also understand the

learning process, how emotions are a big factor, and that modeling patience *teaches* patience.

My friends, the Utah coaches, have stepped into this humorous and real practice of shrugging off the bad turns and off-days. They feel strongly that it's helped them evolve. They are happier; their athletes are livelier; and the team is outstanding. Personal and professional evolution helps our athletes. Coaching can be serious in terms of requiring safety, quality performance, and strict standards to compete and advance. But does it mean when an athlete falls or misses that we need to get tense and mad? When they drop a pass or flub a goal, do we need to yell at them in anger? I don't think so. I believe in wisdom and patience. I believe in standards and strategies. I believe in a coaching evolution that is person-centered, that *shakes hands* with mistakes and *trusts* the process. When we say "Okay," we see the fight and desire in our athletes, and then we guide them to release tension, let go of failure, and strive toward success.

Positive Psychology is Inspiring an Evolution

The more patience and positivity we add, the less negativity the athlete hears—and the easier they can move on after failure. If you want your athlete to let go of the angry voice in their head and generate *good feelings* so they will perform well, then trust their desire and the process. Perhaps your background in sports has taught you to keep applying pressure. I hope you rethink it. Because too much pressure can wear down an athlete to a horrible, defeated mindset. They second guess and doubt their abilities. In that scenario, you will lose much more than you gain.

Healthy minds and athletes are developed through patience and perspective. And they still produce success, and possibly *more*. This is a huge shift because classic coaching viewed mild responses as soft and too tolerant.

But seeking wellness and wisdom in sports is not "soft," it's smart…and **healthy.** *There's no* **less** *effort, or no* **less** *focus for the athlete. In fact, athletes focus more with a positive approach because there's no fear of an upset coach, or having to please a watchful parent. With patience and positivity, athletes have* **more** *energy and focus to improve their moves and plays.*

When you remove the negative emotions there's no quick reaction, no reminding the athlete, "You're still messing up," or asking, "What's wrong with you?"

Success is always desired, but it is illusive; except when you consider success is a great learning experience for a happy athlete. Young or old, any athlete who is motivated will come back the next day and work harder. Making mistakes is important to learning; it's part of training to have bad days and practice resilience. Inspire athletes in the middle of their struggle. Believe in that power.

When Athletes Stand Around...

At times, to get an athlete's attention, it can be appropriate in sports to use a firm or a loud voice. But the truth is, so can a whisper. Have you tried it? Balance your approach. Try something new. Your athletes will pay attention *more*. In looking at the terrible court case of violated athletes, I listened closely to their impact statements where they described their emotional pain and gave detailed accounts of being verbally and emotionally abused in sports. Fear and confusion beat them down and caused incredible vulnerability where they were targeted by a predator. Even in our everyday coaching and parenting, we need to think *deeply* about the words we use and how they impact an athlete. We are walking in an important time of change. So, let's consider this topic as urgent.

In a coaching clinic I presented in California for a large sports program, the coaches were fully engaged and listening. They spoke up and expressed some of their frustrations with certain athletes; that some kids were moving slowly, standing around and not being productive. A few coaches were exasperated, not knowing what to do. So, I paused, and I strongly suggested that when an athlete is standing around, not being productive (maybe "camping out"), please don't say, "You're wasting time." They all paid attention. I emphasized that that statement is extremely negative. Saying these words, *You're wasting time*, is

1. An accusation

2. Not motivating

3. Not accurate because there can be many reasons why an athlete is not doing something, mainly fear. If they are laughing, acting aloof, or distracted, getting drinks of water, going to the bathroom and going slowly, these are coping mechanisms. They are worried or afraid.

4. And if a parent is pushing them to be on the team or in the sport, then I would be empathic and want to help.

Young people do *not* easily have the tools to solve their emotional problems and just follow instructions, "do it," or "go for it." There is no *Emotions 101* in our school system, that I know of. We need to teach them. Athletes are intimidated by coaches, fearful of getting an eye-roll, or chastised for saying, "I'm afraid," or "I can't do it." Overall, they are young! They need strategies and tools. They need our help.

It's not just younger athletes, either. A seventeen-year-old or college athlete may not feel confident or able to articulate what's going on inside them emotionally. Look at the victims of the 2018 sexual abuse case. They could not convince anyone they were being hurt and they were desperately afraid. Consider patience. Consider options. Give the athlete something else to do that will make them feel successful. Compliment their bravery in being at practice, even when they are struggling. Talk about the person, their value as a person, and offer them tools to move forward. We can do this! Let them know you are right there with them. Teach mental and emotional awareness. We are part of the solution of the abuse. And we are creating human greatness.

Human Greatness!

Human connection hooks kids and keeps them coming back. Often, it keeps the coaches coming back, too. We ache for a bond, a partnership, where the inner-workings of our thoughts and emotions allow us to relate to each other. Another element that keeps us all captivated: watching or experiencing *human greatness*. And what I'm referring to is that extraordinary human spirit inside all of us that rises up when facing a challenge. In an athlete's mind, they recognize they can do a skill or move superfast, with power, or artistry, and they feel awesome! Amazing! It's a natural high. We see athletes behind in a race, down, losing…and then make an incredible triumph! We feel the heaviness of an injured athlete, struggling to come back, overcoming immense obstacles, and then climbing back to compete again. We hear crazy-bad referee calls, we feel confused and frustrated, and yet see our children learning to accept "bad calls" and refocus on the next play. We watch coaches who put in long, sweaty days and months of hard work, then talk to the team and trust one athlete to make the last play of a championship game…and score. Some days, we see miracles. We are moved by the good in parents and coaches. We witness grand character and moral heroes who demonstrate greatness through making sacrifices, giving extra time, and teaching life lessons. We say to ourselves, "Wow, that's incredible…I want *that* for my athlete." The personal connection is deep and magical and drives us to participate and keep going. It's an amazing *feeling* to see our young people as athletes, striving and reaching for goals.

Internal Rewards

Athletes want a trophy—who doesn't? I know this intimately. (At age 11, I got all googly-eyed at a District Championship while looking at the shiny trophies lined up on the table. Even before the competition started, my heart began to race!) But trophies are so easy to see with our eyes. That can be a huge distraction. Come on, let's focus! The truth is (are you ready for it?) there's nothing better than the *internal* rewards and the *inner* experience. Because it's a *daily feeling* of being on top of the world (which leads to confidence and, sure, yes, trophies). If you haven't experienced these amazing inner rewards yourself, or used it in coaching, this is powerful stuff. Powerful stuff!

Inner Reward System

Focus on these four actions and recognitions to produce mental and emotional vitality!

- Validation
- Contribution
- Greater Purpose
- Strength through Unity.

Use this system to create ways to heighten your athletes' spirit! This system can also be used at home or with any group of people (volunteers, staff, supporters). Everyone feels better when they are noticed for doing good. With your honesty and alacrity, you will prompt human greatness.

1. **Validate an athlete's talent:** *You have a mighty powerful kick. Good job, keep doing it.*

2. **Salute a Contribution to the team:** *We were behind, and Joe's aggressive play gave the assist and got us tied up. It was smart and a super effort for the team! Thanks, Joe!*

3. **Induce a Greater Purpose:** *Ben has been injured and down for months, then he saw your performance. Watching you inspired him; it made him believe he can do anything.*

4. **Generate Strength through Unity:** *All of us doing sprints at once, I could feel the strength and power of everyone. We're such an awesome team.*

Words and mindful communication are the essence of our inner reward system. Not trophies or medals. The main reasons athletes train hard revolve around *people and emotions*. We find a deeper connection to ourselves and others that is much more valuable than money or titles.

In the coach–athlete relationship, the ***internal rewards*** resonate at the highest level. When we validate and listen to athletes, that means they matter. It's our job to help them develop their self-knowledge and sense of worth. It's a day-by-day process through physical training that we, as coaches and parents, promote inner rewards. And from inside each of us, we make choices through what we value. Values are at our core and we can connect and inspire when we are in tune with what's most important to us.

Values Have Impact

Whatever consumes your mind, you project that every day, every hour, every minute. From our thoughts, we emit attitudes and beliefs. From thoughts, we shape the coach-athlete relationship.

If you didn't realize it, your thoughts and attitude determine what type of success is possible. Really. I'll say it again: Your thoughts and attitude determine what type of success is possible.

In the coach-athlete relationship, athletes learn about us as people, and respond based on how they perceive us. Do you know how athletes perceive you or think about you? Do you know how you impact them?

As we guide and teach, it's helpful to understand how we effect and influence others. That way, we can decide to change and use new strategies. This type of learning is not technical. It's personal. Do you like the values that *your* coach or parents taught you? Have you taken time and formed your own value system *inside your own mind?* Please consider…

- What personal values guide you in the choices you make?
- Do you have a value that helps you pause when you feel uncomfortable or perceive a risk?
- Is patience important to you? Do you begin practice thinking, *I want to be patient…?*

We are complex human beings and yet there's a simplicity to leading with core values. I love athletes and I love to coach them. When we seek connection and happiness in the process, we lift them up and ourselves. Much of it begins with our values.

Your Values

There are different types of values that shape our beliefs and conduct. To create an intention to learn about yourself: 1) Place a check-mark next to all that stand out as important. 2) Circle the ones you want to improve on to be a better coach or support for athletes.

Integrity	Kindness	Forgiveness
Inner peace	Humility	Education
Humor	Acceptance	Hard work
Caring	Gratitude	Organized
Wisdom	Teamwork	Safety
Respect	EmotionalAwareness	Health (phys/mentl)
Inclusion	Relationships	Empathy
Optimism	Open-minded	Courage
Patience	Success	Honesty

Exercise: Top-top Values

There are 36 to choose from. Select 10 values that are most important to you—the ones that resonate with you. Look them over. Do they provide a good variety for your needs and what you believe? Now, from that group, narrow it down. Choose your top 5 values. I know, it's not easy. But this can clarify for you what is truly important in the way you live, coach, and put yourself out in the world. Do you have your top 5…? It may change in six months. We keep evolving. This is a practice to know yourself and solidify a foundation in working with athletes.

Now Make a Sign!

Write your values on a piece of paper and post it on a wall, in your office, a locker room, or in the hallway. Tell your family and friends. Come on, I dare you. And…share with your athletes.

When you live through your values with intention, you are thoughtful. You are a role model. Daily, you are calmly and respectfully guiding your athletes' character by sharing what's important to you. We can help develop their character and values and form a closer bond. This deep human connection gives them power, and you are now developing as partners.

Ask Daily Connection-Questions

Here are clear-cut questions to ask athletes. As you ask, think of them, listen to them, and connect. *Done frequently,* these interactions keep athletes engaged, feeling important, and gives them power. Write these questions down and practice using them, daily. Do not be distracted. Give your athletes your full attention. Be personal and have fun!

1. How are you?

2. What's going on in your life?

3. What do you want to accomplish or get out of today's practice?

4. What do you think you need to do?

5. How can I help you?

Reading these questions is a start. Now, practice. Yes, right now. Ask out loud. "How are you?" "What's going on in your life" "What do you want to accomplish?" "Oh! And what do you think?" Just like your athletes doing their repetitions in sprints or pushups or other drills, you need to practice your *human connection drills.* Ask...listen...and by my "human calculations," you are tapping into wisdom...and a phenomenal partnership!

CHAPTER 4

Let's Be Partners

I won't let you down, even when you struggle.
I will lift you up.

Power Balance

We. *We are in this together.* Have you said *that* to your athletes? Because right now, you have the power. You have the opportunity to shift the power from you…to both of you. And they need it. When athletes feel that unified energy from you, it gives them a sense of forces joining. It's not "kids vs. adults," or "athletes vs. coaches." Tell them, *"We're in this together."*

To be clear, there's been a power-imbalance in sports, an unhealthy, sometimes scary one. For any adult who's misused their power—perhaps trapped in old habits—athletes don't have a choice. They must follow and can't speak up. "Power-over" has been the monster and manipulator, and if not from us, we have seen it and stood by. What I hear, read, and witness, we've all been tolerant. Parents don't always recognize it, but many have said things to me, like "We don't want to upset the coach," or "The coach likes my son, but he won't let him play." Parents feel disheartened because there's no discussion; it's 100% the coach's thought process and decision. No discussion about timing or the coach's thought process and decision. And sometimes, the parent exudes the power. Ultimately, parent, coach, and athlete on the same track will best support the athlete in their journey and increase the positive energy all around them.

This chapter emphasizes the coach-athlete partnership, and *integral* to that is the parent's role in the partnership model with coach and athlete. Plus, the support of many *sports partners* (i.e., trainer, physical therapist, strength coach, mental training coach, nutritionist) is critical.

Many partners can boost the overall experience and success and keep the athlete safe—when there is open communication and cooperation.

So, whether it's subtle or obvious, *we all need to look within ourselves.* Don't be silent. Talk and influence healthy relationships by empowering athletes as your partner: Speak, share ideas, listen, and make adjustments. Avoid heavy emotion or negative pressure that demeans. There is respect for each other with encouragement, honesty, and integrity. And that's the beginning of a powerful partnership that will thrive!

Childhood Stories

On one of my travels, I spent time with some coaches and their team in Colorado. I was coaching a clinic, and take note, my clinics are a little unusual. I don't just teach tools…I get *very personal.* Revealing our inner selves is part of the learning process, so we go deep. I gazed at a group of twenty fabulous athletes, smiled and asked, "Who holds their feelings inside? Who holds their feelings inside sometimes, or a lot? Who stuffs them down and won't tell your coaches when you're confused, frustrated, or in pain?" Hands flew up! About fifteen openly confessed that they keep everything inside. I replied, "Yeahh…that's normal. Athletes want to be 'tough,'" I said.

Then, one coach interrupted: "Wait, wait, let's go back to that. We are a friendly program, we're positive, very open, we talk and listen a lot. I don't understand why they would stuff down their feelings and hold them inside." The coach was flabbergasted.

What happened next was really cool. I explained there are many reasons *why*. You see, athletes "hold in," their feelings because of:

- needing to be perfect
- the "loser mentality," comparing, noticing teammates are ahead and they are not
- worried if they aren't "tough," then they're "weak"
- But the *biggest reason* athletes hold in feelings is because *WE ARE THE AUTHORITY*

We are. Coaches are the authority; the *power* is always with us. Athletes have none. For them, that lack of power causes resistance, intimidation, and doubt. So, they hide their feelings from us.

In order to change this dynamic, to free athletes to be more open and help them through their emotions, we need to promote a **Power Balance.**

I spoke to the coaches and went on... "If you share a childhood story, something the athletes don't know about you, like when you felt vulnerable or made a poor decision. *That allows the athletes to see you just like them. Like kids.*" The two coaches' eyes widened, "Really? Okay." They took turns telling stories to their team. One coach said she didn't like the way she looked and that she had skinny legs and felt insecure. The other coach, as a boy, had gotten mad at his parents and did a bad thing. He got in trouble and ran away from home (for an hour). It was hilarious. We all laughed, and the athletes admitted they didn't know any of that about their coaches. This was an amazing connection. The team got a dose of their coaches as human beings, as young people *without power.* It was a moment of equality.

Power Balance is a working relationship where both sides, athlete and coach, feel they share and contribute equally in the training process.

I will emphasize, for the athletes, they are largely guided by adults, of course, but this feeling of equality gives them a voice and identity that, in every way, *they matter*. It fuels a strong sense of freedom and courage for athletes they don't otherwise have. Both partners make decisions—and they also make mistakes. They take turns with new ideas, and through thick and thin, show respect for each other. Even with the coach as a guide, as an older, more knowledgeable person in sports, the athlete feels they are "in it together" and have equal say. This is a true partnership in action. There's no doubt, athletes *will* perform better!

Boys

Boys are not excluded. They need and thrive in a positive partnership. They tend to be brief in expressing themselves, but be sure, they have deep feelings. One point, for which I am resolute, is that no one should *ever* expect boys to "hold it in." The old adage "boys don't cry," or "never show weakness," is wrong. It's inhuman and destructive and a major problem in sports and how we raise young men with high self-esteem and emotional intelligence. So let's change. Power balance is *absolutely* necessary. By opening up communication with personal stories, you're giving permission to be vulnerable and human…and the guys will appreciate it.

Exercise: Coaches Tell Stories

You don't need to be Mark Twain, just be you. Flaws and mistakes are real and relatable. When you're talking, go back in your mind to the vivid emotions you felt. Tell sad, frustrating, or happy stories. The best are humorous. But athletes also need to understand we have struggled and we can relate to them. After you tell yours, invite team members to comment. Always take turns and be careful of teasing. All comments should be sincere. This practice of sharing and trusting is amazing. Time allowance: thirty-minute talks can transform. Shoot, take an hour! The time investment gives you weeks of more confident athletes, I swear. Post the planned meeting on a board/calendar where all can see, and send everyone an email a week in advance and two days before. The athletes will be curious! Meet every two to four weeks, change the topic to sports heroes or reasons you admire your team. Then, watch the bond and focus rise.

In this time of abuse awareness, while coaches are wondering how to motivate their teams, we can connect in a positive, healthy way. At gyms, courts, ice rinks and on fields, the work and setting can be structured, productive, and a happy, safe place for athletes. If you think about it, the act of creating a partnership is a sacred space in their minds. Sacred in realizing their dreams. The heart of that dream is their trusting relationship with you—their Partner.

The Partner

In a positive partnership model, each person honors the other as an important contributor. This approach to coaching and parenting is highly effective, safer, and very motivating for athletes.

The Partnership Model™

ATHLETE
Talent & Desire
Personal Knowledge
Positivity & Diligence
Powerful Voice
Authenticity

Shared
Values
& Goals

Mutual
Kindness
& Respect

COACH
Sports Knowledge
Vision & Inspiration
Health/Safety Advocate
Collaborative Planning
Transparency

PARENT
Unconditional Love
Wisdom & Guidance
Health/Safety Advocate
Calming Presence
Fun & Optimism

Thoughtful
Communication

Qualities and Steps to Collaborate and Partner Successfully

In every way, positive partners celebrate the athlete as a whole person, striving toward achievement in sports and happiness in life. A partner conveys confidence and a feeling of safety to the athlete through their ongoing support. Daily.

A Positive Partner

- Makes the learning process positive and gets athletes to say, "I can!" in a challenge. Shake hands with your athlete, and say, "I believe in you." Invigorate the partnership.

- Confirms shared values and talks about common goals with a smile and sure voice.

- Knows that each partner controls *only themselves*. There's no power-over, no forcing, no internal link to make your athlete "hit a homer." You are separate and you can observe.

- Walks in to practices and views the athlete as an intelligent collaborator. They continually learn *how* to work together best, without yelling, blame, or diminishing someone's spirit.

- Understands that only the athlete can feel what's happening to their body. Only the athlete knows what's going on inside their mind. Only the athlete feels fear and doubt rising up inside of them. Listen to each other to be safe and productive.

- Recognizes when things are complicated, rushed, or confusing and slows down when an athlete needs it. A partner also perceives when it's time to advance.

- Is patient with struggles, keeps an open mind, ready to try something new to help the athlete.

- Establishes respectful communication with important rules and precautions, and includes parents for an open conversation when there are challenges or concerns. Always transparent.

- Practices fairness and does not choose favorites or isolate athletes. A partner advocates for safety, team harmony, and handling all issues with positive hearts and minds.

- Is complimentary and values other people's wisdom; seeks knowledge for ongoing progress.

- Works with transparency and regularly reviews the timeline, progress update, and strategies to stay on track for reaching goals. Never as pressure; simply to inform.

You *know* competitive sports are very challenging. In the hardest physical training sessions, athletes hurt: they cramp up, huff and puff, get sore and shaky, yet they want to please the coach.

It's our role to help athletes learn about their own limits: when to push, when to stop, when they cramp, or something hurts. They need to listen to their bodies. During tough workouts, coaches can compliment efforts, and say, "You are strong and brave, and I appreciate you." *In this way, you will help build confidence and success.*

When sensitive issues need to be addressed, plan and present it respectfully with parents or other coaches. Partners consider a neutral location, or allow the athlete to be present and let them sit behind the coach's desk. Give the athlete the power!

Ways to Coach and Teach Tiny Details

Be specific and athletes will get it! Connect on an emotional level, and athletes will become more focused. To heighten physical performance, here are a few tips in speaking to your athletes in the *Partnership* model…

1. When athletes need to perform a precise movement, it helps to focus *exactly* on their bodies, their positions, and *how* they want to move. Ask questions like, "Do you feel your leg kicking straight?" "Can you show me how far you want your arm to reach?" Make it clear and basic so they can interact with you. If you just say, "Go harder," that doesn't teach.

2. I tell young athletes, "Talk to your body. Tell your foot, 'Kick straight!' and tell your legs, 'Jump high!'" and the kids smile really big. They begin to think in terms of focusing and communicating with themselves. This begins better communication for you as a Partner. And they feel more comfortable talking to you about their form and movements.

3. If an athlete appears nervous, ask them, "When you are about to make that play, what do you want to say to yourself before you do it?" In this way, you're helping athletes understand they program their minds, and both of you can brainstorm self-talk and strategies, together.

4. Let the athlete teach YOU something. Be very patient, respectful and fully supportive. This teaching moment could be as simple as a correct push-up or a combination of moves. When an athlete gets to coach the coach (and the coach pretends to be the athlete), you both experience something amazing. You have switched roles and you *trust* each other—you trust your athlete is smart enough to teach, your athlete trusts that you care enough to listen.

Just Trust the Universe

Alan Watts says, "The way to become one with the universe....is to trust it."

When you exert power to control *someone or something, you actually* lose *power. I will say it again: When you exert power to control someone or something, you actually lose power. But the more you* give *power and share it—there is a flow of energy—and you have* more *power.*

To have harmony and unity and forward motion toward common goals, a person cannot assert power over another. We can, though, instruct, observe, and listen. We can delegate authority and check in on the progress. We can have unity as "coach-athlete" or "parent-athlete" when we release control, combine our power...and trust.

This is not an idea or a concept, this *is* a human experience. In sports, in a power balance, it's not "you" or "I" in control of the other, which is a separation of energy and intention. You are together (minds and hearts) working toward the same goal. Create this by valuing the synergy between you.

The hardest task ever is to let go, not have control, to trust another and trust the process. When it comes to a young athlete who has great ability, yet they are resisting and struggling, it's difficult to trust that moment. I know. But I believe, as you keep reading, you are learning to enjoy the present moment. And I believe you have enormous power to give to your athletes. So, help them embrace every challenge together. You can do it!

The Self-defeating Habit

I coach athletes in mental training. It's my job and I love it. All athletes self-defeat with inner negativity and doubts, from beginning competitors to the pros. So how do you help them? Here's a tip: Follow their emotions by observing them...and be patient.

Let's observe. One athlete I coached was anxious for months and emotionally broke down in waves of tears in practice multiple times. Another athlete became hard and quiet, highly self-critical, and couldn't produce a solid practice. A third was sad, felt excluded, and isolated herself. She felt very alone. These athletes are driven and highly competitive. But they self-criticize and self-sabotage. They struggle to feel good about themselves, and they even feel *unworthy*. During our mental training sessions, they opened up to me and began to notice how they were self-defeating. So, I suggested that we create a plan for change. They liked the optimism in having clear action steps and techniques to shift their thoughts and emotions. After that, they applied my suggestions and reported wonderful improvements and great practices. This does not happen overnight, because mental training requires time and repetitions. But each athlete practiced and learned self-awareness, how to reprogram their minds, and take control.

What athletes tell me is true.

The pressure to not miss, perform with precision, score, or finish fast, and be successful in competition is overwhelming. Because most athletes only feel valuable when they have success—and when the coach sees it. The problem is they believe their worthiness is based on whether they can perform.

We don't think about it daily, but athletes are frequently afraid of being judged and rejected. It's true in sports and at home. Many times, athletes tell me their thoughts overpower them and they worry or freak out! They ache for approval. They are desperate to be liked and to be *someone*.

The Good News, Infusing Good Feelings

Positive human connection with a coach enhances the athlete's sense of self-value, that they are worthy, they are good, and they can do it. It's important to infuse athletes with good feelings. Now, you can't control their feelings, but you can *influence* through care. Take these steps...

1. Recognize that your athletes often struggle from inherent pressures, even when you don't notice it. You can't change it, but you can lighten it with your approach.

2. Offer genuine care and connection with your words and patience, "I know this is hard but I'm right here; I will help you. We can do this together."

3. Celebrate the heck out of their persistence and efforts. Show enthusiasm and belief in their abilities! Jump up and down, give high fives, write positive words on a white board.

4. Say these words: "You're great. You can do it. I KNOW you can do it. Keep at it. We're working together." They need to hear it from you when they are trying but feeling like they're in the tunnel of mental endurance.

5. When you see them struggle say, "Let's take a breath...good. Take your time. That was a good effort. What can we learn from that? Okay, we'll get this tomorrow." Don't talk about results, keep their mind in the positive present moment of learning.

Exercise: Teach Success with "I Can!"

Ask your athletes, "Who can...?" and they'll be curious and usually blurt out, "I CAN! I CAN!" before you finish. They get big eyes, hands shoot up. Give mid-level challenges where athletes will succeed. Have them repeat what they did well. What did you do? "I straightened my legs. I jumped high. I followed through." These phrases are the same as "I can" in technical words. It builds an inner dialogue of what they *can do* and what they do well. Finally, especially for teens, you can help them dissolve their fears of limitation. Because they create walls and they don't feel worthy. But your words help. Say, "You are an awesome person. And you *can* accomplish your goals. Forget the negative people. Forget them." (Spit and stomp if needed.) Because it stinks

when others try to bring young people down. We need to build them up! With your patience and positivity, celebrate and connect…and it starts. Athletes will begin to feel worthy, develop self-esteem, and improve in practices. The more you immerse athletes into your world and your positive words and feelings, the messages sink into their own mind…and they rise.

Words Stick

An athlete needs to feel confident in practice and say to themselves over and over, "I can do this! I'm strong! I'm gonna nail this." But the biggest issue is many coaches have a habit of saying things like, "No, do it again," or "No, you're too slow," "You keep making the same mistake," "We're going to stay on this drill until you make five." The message athletes get: No. No. I keep making mistakes. Stay…I keep failing. Words stick in their minds. What coaches and parents can become more aware of is the balance of pushing an athlete to improve (which challenges them) and acknowledging their effort and strengths (which focuses on the positive). Too many notes on the critical mistakes does *not* build confidence. It builds negative self-talk.

I have two sons. They played Pop Warner (tackle) football. Players from ages six to sixteen practiced hard and played for the Vikings from August to November. I was a Viking mom for six years. I also have a daughter. My jock-daughter played three years (believe it or not)—full pads, helmet, tackle football—she was the girl on the football team. I wasn't thrilled at first, my girl getting hit and tackled, but she was strong and fast. Determined like no one else. I also knew the coaches, and I listened to their messages. They were all about safety, encouragement, and team spirit. Those messages trickled down to parents and players. We felt like family.

My daughter is grown up now, in college. I asked her what she liked about playing football and what sticks in her mind the most. You know what she recalled? She said, "I remember opponents at games seeing me and saying to my teammates with a sneer: *You gotta girl on your team?* And the boys stood up for me. They said, *Yeah…and you better watch out. She's* fast."

Words stick.

CHAPTER 5
I Won't Be Too Hard on You
All persons of authority can learn a new approach.
Athletes deserve to feel protected and safe.

Present moment. Live in the present moment. When you do, everything else falls away, stress leaves us, and inspiration comes. We don't realize it sometimes, but we are distracted with the past and the future, we tense up, and then we push athletes too hard. From five feet away, or miles away, coaches, parents, and decision makers affect young people. They get nervous and don't feel safe. This chapter is real. Let's learn to be present and thoughtful every single day. Practice empathy and look deeply into your athlete's eyes. Think about what's best for them. We can do this with our highest intention. Together.

Adult Lens vs. Child Lens

A group of young athletes were traveling in a van with their coach. From California to Arizona, after a competition, it was still light out. There were six girls in the van: an eleven-year-old, and the others were 14-16. All of a sudden, on the highway, the coach pulls over. He says, "Everyone needs to improve on conditioning, so you're going to run." He tells them to get out of the van. "I'm going to drive up the road about two miles and wait for you there."

They needed to run.

Alone, on an open highway, six girls ran a couple miles…till they reached the van. These young athletes were physically fine, but inside there was no security. They were completely vulnerable.

This is a true story. The woman who told me was one of the girls in the van and had to run. As I listened, my jaw dropped. I don't doubt for a second that the coach just thought about conditioning and running— like at a school, gym, or field, and the athletes were capable—but for the athletes this was incredibly scary. And dangerous. Anyone driving by could have stopped and approached them. The fact is, they knew their coach's personality; they felt pressured to comply with "random assignments" in the past. And on that day, running two miles, they must have been terrified to be out there alone with no adult nearby.

What I'm emphasizing is the difference between the adult lens and the athlete lens and how we have such unbelievable power over them.

Not one athlete spoke up. No one said, *No, I'm uncomfortable. No, it's not safe. Coach, I don't want to do that.* If they had, they would've been chastised, embarrassed, and on the bad side of the coach. He might have had them run farther.

What is imperative, of course, is safety, but also consider the athlete's emotional experience. How afraid they were to get out of the van…or stay in the van. When we tell them to do something, they usually do it. And when we only think of a task, and not the emotional impact it will have, then we are *disconnected* from reality…and from the athletes.

Slow Down and Think

Goals, time, and urgency rush us and disconnect us from our athletes' essential needs. Keep in mind every athlete has important psychological and emotional needs (see Chapter 3). Your guidance and encouragement will be more impactful when *you* "go inward" and connect to your emotional intelligence with understanding and empathy.

Now, consider what type of coach or parent you want to be. We have all developed tendencies, attitudes, and mannerisms, and this is the best time to reflect and look at yours. I never want to place blame on anyone's habits, but rather support you in ways to learn, transform, and build a new culture in sports. Let's take a look. Don't rush through this. To develop a clear vision and intention of what you want, this takes thought. Slow down…and think for a while. Take notes. Create your best self, create your working relationship with athletes, and consider how they are impacted by you.

Identify the Severe Approach

The Ruler

The strict disciplinarian has been a historic coaching model in our sports culture—for both males and females. This severe type of behavior in coaches, parents, or any adult, will be referred to as "the Ruler." For the Ruler, their greatest desire is to be in control. Rulers want to be seen as the boss, they want athletes to keep quiet, and they insist on doing things one way. The Ruler is the total authority and has all the knowledge, controlling everyone from the "I" and "my." This is called "my way." "My way" is the highway (sometimes, literally) and it's scary. "My way" only considers the thoughts, feelings, and power of the Ruler. No questions…the athlete obeys.

A Ruler's Tendencies & Habits Hurt and Weaken Athletes

You can become alert to the emotional pains of an athlete by recognizing this behavior in detail. These behaviors may not show up every day, which can be confusing, so watch for certain patterns and speak up when you believe an athlete or team is in a vulnerable or risky position.

Over time, the Ruler makes it easier for predators to target our athletes. So, remember, this knowledge is to be shared and talked about with athletes, so they can feel in charge.

Learn that the Ruler:

- Uses commanding language or frequently exudes intimidation: *"I'm the coach. You are the athlete. I know the sport. I am older, smarter, and I know how to train and win. I tell you what to do and you will follow. If you want to win, you must do it. If you complain, you're out."*

- Talks more about winning, and often it's the only goal. This is ego-centered and derives from a fear of failing. The Ruler's value and reputation rely on their athletes' success.

- Shifts moods depending on the athlete's performance. Daily, it is the athlete's job to please the coach. If athletes do not perform to the highest standard, then they get scolded and belittled. Athletes are typically nervous to upset the coach or make any kind of mistake.

- Acts as judge, jury, and executioner. If athletes don't do everything just so, they are punished and made to feel like a coward. This is a fixed environment and constantly hammers on the athlete's psyche, creating shame and vulnerability.

- Appears and sounds powerful, maybe even confident, but their dominance actually confuses, frightens, and weakens an athlete, tears them down mentally and emotionally.

- Rarely gives compliments or praise. Athletes rarely feel good enough—not even as a person.

- Intimidates and keeps secrets. What the Ruler says and does is often in private, never questioned, not shared or up for discussion. It's a secret.

In sports for both boys and girls, the Ruler's approach is hurtful and one-sided, demanding the athlete to conform. Only the toughest hang in there and survive, yet many are typically damaged for years. This is a tactic of power-over and lacks everything related to the humanistic approach.

When a coach or parent dismisses an athlete's experience, intelligence, and feelings in front of others, he/she manipulates everyone around them. When athletes are restricted and scared to speak up, fear and pain become normal and familiar. Fear and pain, unconsciously, become acceptable.

It is my hope we will *not continue* to see this behavior, but it takes every single coach and parent to not only reflect on themselves, but to speak up. The Ruler's behavior is abusive and manipulative, and athletes cannot manage it, let alone thrive. At best, they endure. We can all become aware, we can all change, and we can do it, now.

Exercise: What Do You Want to Change?

Pause and reflect... Have you received some feedback about your words and behavior? Have you felt criticized, and if so, can any of it be true? Is there room for you to improve as a coach or parent? Even the smallest change can make a big difference. Get a pen and let's begin!

1. Write down habits you can consider changing in yourself, below.

2. Then go back to the *Partner* qualities and steps in Chapter 4 and add a short plan of your new approach. Start with your intention to be the best you, and to have positive impact with your athletes.

3. Write new phrases and ways to acknowledge your athletes' efforts. Even when you're tired or busy, prioritize the athletes, find ways to compliment and encourage them.

_____

_____

_____

_____

Bring Your Highest Energy & Inspire

Few coaches are the Ruler to the maximum de-
gree, but we all have habits and areas to improve.
Because we get tired, distracted, preoccupied, or
overwhelmed with concerns in our lives. Sometimes, you just want to take a nap for three days!
I know! But it's critical to be aware when you're
tired and patience and mindfulness are not present. To focus and partner with athletes, we all

BURNT OUT

need to attend to personal issues and set aside our "stuff." Drop it
at the door! Especially while coaching. Because when we choose to
coach, it is a choice to serve.

If you find yourself checking your phone, thinking about a relationship,
or finances, then perhaps you need to take time to attend to them. For

ENERGIZED

work issues on your mind, set up a meeting and
talk it out. Clarify with your boss what is most
important to you. If for any reason, you feel extra
tense, worn down, or your job feels like survival,
then it's a problem.

Take a breath right now...inhale...and exhale...
Connect with higher-mind thinking. Practice
awareness of your intentions to teach and inspire,
and bring your highest energy and focus to guiding your athletes.
Coaching and parenting should be thought-full, not thought-less. Do

you want to inspire athletes to be their best? Absolutely! Then arrive to each moment as rested as possible. Eat healthy, think grateful thoughts, and bring *your best* for them. You will enjoy your interactions with athletes and have more impact when you are focused and organized in your mind. Most of all, consider the athlete's experience so they will feel happy and safe. They will have difficult days with emotions, even tears, and they need your patience and support.

Crying: Coaches Can Handle It Wisely

My favorite type of work is in person talking, teaching, listening; that's where I'm most alive and having fun. I'm also in some coaching groups online. I check in from time to time; I like the diverse topics, chatter, and considering other views than my own. There are some very thoughtful comments, and there are reactive comments. Overall, this is another way I'm in the world of sports and in tune with what's happening. One day, on the subject of crying, a coach was frustrated. With one short post of frustration—about an athlete expressing sadness and disappointment through tears—and quickly there was an onslaught of comments and statements from other coaches all over the country. I was confounded.

Do You Get Upset by Athletes' Emotions?

Coach Complaints	How Coach is perceived
I get mad at them when they cry at practice.	Coach sounds emotional, too!
If they aren't happy with a medal or ribbon, I'll be happy to take it from them and they don't need to worry about it.	Coach is distant, impatient
I can't get my athletes to do anything, like show a good attitude when they don't win.	Little influence or authority

Parents coddle the kids. What life lessons are they teaching?	Coach is angry with parents
I tell them to stop or they go home!	Threatening
My athlete started to cry at awards, had a bad attitude, so I told the athlete in front of the team it was unacceptable and she was now suspended for two weeks.	Total reaction & humiliation

"Don't cry" is common in sports. I know. I was an athlete who was told, "Crying's not allowed." After the age of eleven I kept such control over my emotions. In the car or at home, my mom was there for me, but I was taught to respect the coach's authority, follow instructions. And she didn't understand that type of sports pressure and I couldn't really explain it. I was too young. So, I often held it inside, thinking I needed to be tough, anyway. Psychologists recommend healthy support for emotions, and do not recommend this *rule* of "no crying." I strongly urge parents and coaches to be smarter, wiser, and educate athletes about feelings and how to manage them. Talk about emotions. Teach them emotional awareness and emotional intelligence. (See "Emotions Chart" in Chap 1)

Prepare Athletes: Crying is a human expression—*human.* We cry for many reasons, like sadness, fear, anxiety, frustration, disappointment, feeling rejected, even total excitement and joy.

Tears are a release of emotions and toxins and create a balance in our minds and bodies. Tears are human **and important!**

Athletes often hold in their feelings, so teach them that tears are okay and healthy; they can go to the bathroom or locker room if they want privacy for a moment. If they do not express tears/emotion, they become a big ball of worry and tension, and their performance will suffer. In sports, let's be real and talk about how and when it's appropriate to express emotions. At the beginning of a training season, it's helpful to present a series of short talks to share philosophies and educate athletes on the process of training and competing.

Season Preparation Talk

1. Prepare the athletes for your expectations: how you will all work together, and what the group can decide for a team goal.

2. Explain that this is their experience and they can ask for help at any time. You care about them and their voice matters.

3. Talk about *tough workouts*. Practices are meant to be productive, and some will be tough. I tell young athletes, "Some days your bodies will feel tired, your muscles might cramp up, and you may cry. But that means you're getting stronger." (Athletes like to hear "you're getting stronger.") I continue, "If you're hurt or need extra help, I'm right here. But when you work hard, you have the best chance of reaching your goals. Do you want to get stronger?" They say, "Yes!" I say, "Great!" And we smile and clap together!

4. Prepare your athletes for competition the same way. Speak to them with respect and fully explain what they will see, feel, and do. Tell them, "I believe in you. If you fall or make mistakes, or if you don't win or get a medal, that's okay, that's sports." Remind them that you will be right there, helping them along the way.

5. Most important is to respect each other and stay positive. Consider adopting a team philosophy, like, "Our intention is to hold our heads high, be proud of our effort, and learn how to improve."

6. Ask them, "Can you explain your idea of character? How can you show good sportsmanship?" Get the athletes to talk about it. Make a poster or something that emphasizes their desire to model good character and sportsmanship.

I understand you don't want a bunch of crying athletes at practices or games. Neither do I. But every once in a while, someone cries. Don't be surprised. If you work with athletes, remember they feel pressure, they are humans with emotions, and be prepared for it.

When Athletes Lose it - Defuse it

When you see an athlete have a breakdown, their emotions seem self-centered and negative. It affects the rest of the team, and *you don't have time to deal with this right now.*

Simple steps to defuse: First, take a moment and recognize their performance is already suffering, or they blew it, they feel confused, their goals start to look hopeless, and suddenly, they feel like *nothing*. Slooowww down and invest thirty seconds to one minute of compassion and empathy. That usually creates a moment of calm and shifts the situation. Consider they may need to step away from practice or, if they are completely overwhelmed, go home. But in that moment, be patient and defuse it. Please...do *not* yell at them. An athlete crying, and an adult yelling is a clash of extreme emotions. Anger is reactive and makes things worse. Certainly, the athlete needs to stop what he/she is doing, take some deep breaths, and change the expectation for the day. If you value good communication and support, then speak after practice to set up a time to talk in the next couple days. Think about what you observed. Think about what you'd like to say. Do not use email or texting. In person is most caring, clear, and appropriate for sensitive matters.

Defuse Emotions and Look Deeper to Help Your Athlete...

1. If you see a pattern of intense emotions, there's likely a deeper issue, beyond sports.

2. Deeper issues require a kind conversation with the athlete and their parent(s).

3. Be sure to say that you're not singling them out, you're not angry or disappointed. You have equal concern for anyone who's struggling.

4. If the behavior appeared as a bad attitude, again, have an open talk. Plan the time to meet and sit down in a professional/safe place away from the practice area.

5. Lead with truth about the behavior: that you wish they weren't struggling but the intense emotions are disruptive. You want to help so they can improve and stay aligned with their goals and the team goals.

6. Be clear about respecting team dynamics, and talk about positive options to work it out in a healthy way. Because something is wrong. It's not just sports.

7. Sometimes a doctor, counselor, or mental training coach is needed. Consider that time off from practice can be a huge help; it can relieve immediate pressure and permit a fresh perspective to return and add more positivity to the team.

One common approach with teenagers is, "Take it outside," which means go to the bathroom or locker room; give the athlete some space away from the team and get it together. *Not as a punishment or humiliation.* But done with respect—allowing the athlete to step away, get space, take some breaths, shake off tension and return with a favorable mindset—this is a healthy way to manage stress and difficult feelings. Always address the positive part of learning to manage these emotional issues. Because every single athlete *needs to manage their emotions.* Not just the athletes who outwardly struggle.

Martha Got Mad

I was working twice a week with an athlete who was struggling, mentally and emotionally. One of her coaches (we'll call her Martha) was not a fan of mental training or anything "Psychology." Hard work was her answer. The athlete was fourteen-years-old and training for an advanced level. Multiple times she had reached the point of quitting; her fears had literally taken over her, she cried often, broke down in practices with the red face and panic, and was terribly scared to do certain skills. In fact, she could not keep up with her teammates for months and her coaches were at a loss. If this girl had a future at all in the sport, she needed intensive mental training. So, we were doing that.

Fortunately, this young athlete "bought in" and is now very successful in her career. But it was months of commitment to train her mind, apply tools, and create new perspectives. All the pressures and expectations, especially from Martha, had added to her emotional struggles. I advised cutting back a little on her regular team training, only because her schedule was so tight, and she needed to increase the mental work to make progress. Martha blew a fuse. "She needs to finish her assignments today!" she yelled at me one day in the middle of a mental training session. (That was uncool.) It was clear to me that Martha did not trust the process. I was unnerved, but I realized she didn't understand that physically, the athlete would never advance without learning to manage her thoughts and feelings. Plus, she didn't feel safe and that was the larger issue. I briefly acknowledged the outburst, then walked away...

A few months later, this brave athlete had gone through a complete transformation. Where she'd been confused, she was clear. Where she had dreaded competition, she enjoyed it. Where she had been unraveled by nerves, she became focused and deliberate in her performances. This young lady was not only brave and persistent but amazed us all. She had a great competition season. Her confidence bloomed. And I am pleased that, not long after that, she earned a full scholarship to a great academic university.

The Question: Was It Working?

Were the regular practices with her coaches helping her reduce her fears and regain her skills? No. They were not. Was Martha supportive of the athlete's emotional well-being? Not in this situation. It's so hard for some coaches when the mental and emotional issues are considerable. Coaches are not required to be trained in psychology or understand emotional issues. I suggest continual professional development for all coaches, and always include a psychological component that teaches human behavior. Meanwhile, it's imperative to be open-minded and trust the athlete's emotions are real (just like a broken bone) and something is seriously wrong. Question: In an emotional spiral with an athlete, would you be able to trust the process in order to create a safe feeling and support that athlete? It will take time, it may take four weeks, eight or twelve, to overcome certain issues and employ new habits. Deep fear or anxiety bids us to be patient, so the athlete can feel more at ease in learning and applying the tools. If you are concerned about the team environment, then a mindset of learning *through* the struggle is needed. Because no one can change from "struggle" to "control" in a split second. No one can feel confident and manage their fears in a week. It is a p-r-o-c-e-s-s. Martha, later, saw the progress…and was surprised.

Coaches Can Evolve

We can transform with higher-mind thinking. We can evolve. We've all made mistakes and said negative things, then walked away from an athlete and thought, "Why did I say that? That wasn't helpful." Since you're reading this book, I believe you'd like to have impact in the most positive way and help athletes to be their best. To be their healthiest. Here, we can learn. Look at a few "sketches" of coaching faux-pas. These are "Do Nots." In order to recognize mental bloopers, it's good to look at them. We are practicing *awareness!* Perhaps you've witnessed these behaviors, in others, or yourself. Analyzing them on all levels can help you identify what to avoid, and more importantly, what you want to do.

Sketch #1: Knows Everything: this person does no wrong and seems to know *everything*, and the athlete knows nothing. Suddenly the athlete's enthusiasm is, zap, gone.

To process this behavior, reflect on your thoughts. Have you observed this attitude? What action can you take to create positive change?

_____

_____

_____

Sketch #2: Sour: rolls-their-eyes-a-lot and has three sharp words, "What was *that*," or "Not even *close*," and just says "No" a lot: "No, do it again." "No, oh my god." "No, how many times have I told you?"

To process this behavior, reflect on your thoughts. Have you observed this attitude? What action can you take to create positive change?

_____

_____

_____

Sketch #3: Yeller: the coach that shoots off orders and consequences, scaring the heck out of everyone around them. Intimidation is a major tool to motivate. Fear is another.

To process this behavior, reflect on your thoughts. Have you observed this attitude? What action can you take to create positive change?

_____

_____

_____

Sketch #4: Quiet: this one can slip by; it's the distracted actions, maybe on their phone, talks quietly to other adults, and then forgets about the athlete, or stares at them…*hard*.

To process this behavior, reflect on your thoughts. Have you observed this attitude? What action can you take to create positive change?

_____

_____

_____

These behaviors are habits, and they are ruled by our ego.

Whenever we feel consumed with frustration or needing to exude power, it's a learned habit. To coach and teach an athlete means we need to coach and teach ourselves, *first.*

Learned Habits: We Don't Mean It, but These Hurt

We've all been taught by someone, many of us in the old tradition of "coach is boss." Now, we have habits. Some good, some not good. Some are *hurtful*. Our intention is to motivate, teach the lesson of pushing through challenges, yet we don't want to hurt athletes. Traditionally, coaches often perceived athletes to be "weak" if they got their feelings hurt: "Toughen up," "Try harder." Our *motivation* can err on the side of using phrases that sound negative. Consider your words and how they impact an athlete. Notice if you think or say the phrases in the left column. Decide to let them go. Humor, patience, and finding connection as partners, this is the way.

Create new thoughts and language. Use examples from the right column.

You're wasting time.	Looks like you're going slow. How can I help you?
How many times have I told you?	This isn't working for you, let's try a new way.
You've got to be kidding me!	You seem unfocused. Let's review the technique?
You're not trying hard enough.	I don't see progress. Tell me what you're thinking.
I don't know what to do with you.	This is challenging. Let's go for pizza.
Look at him, he can do it. Why can't you?	Let's take a breath, together…I know it takes time.
My grandma can run faster.	My grandma was pretty fast. How about yours?

Breathe, Detach, Choose the Present Moment

Thich Naht Hanh is a great, wise Zen Master. He encourages us to pay attention to our breath. He also says the present moment is our "home." That makes perfect sense in sports. We all benefit by taking deep breaths to get calm, and it's key to feel "at home"—in the present moment—at a practice or game. Not in the past, or the future, but

right here, right now, feeling at ease and comfortable. You choose to focus on things that are positive or negative. Ask yourself, *Right here, right now, is anything lacking?* Usually, in the present moment, you have everything you need. And your athletes, in the present moment, have everything they need.

Do this. Breathe *with* your team: Start practice with, "Line up, everyone. Thank you. Today, we're going to practice breathing." Each day for a month, I challenge you to assist the peaceful feeling inside your athletes. Take one deep breath with them, then two, and then a third. It will ground them in their bodies. Release tension. Create a habit of experiencing a calm inner presence. Tell them to use deep breaths to get focused. This is a skill and it takes practice.

Choose a focus: With your athletes, while breathing, pay attention to your bodies filling up with air…and exhaling all the way out. Pay attention to the rhythm, the slowness, and think of a soothing place that brings a smile to your face. Pay attention to this wonderful feeling of being still and calm for a minute or two…just being calm.

The world around us is 90% distraction. Focus on yourself, eyes closed, and put 100% focus on your breath. If your athletes giggle, which they may do, they are not used to it. They don't realize yet the great benefits they'll experience in being mentally clear and performing much better. Teach and practice going inward, practice being self-aware, letting go of everything else. Remind your athletes in training that taking intentional breaths directly relates to focus, confidence, and excelling in sports. So pause, take a breath, and direct your attention on an immediate goal. Take things one-step-at-a-time. Stay in the present moment.

For You, Young Athlete

I see you standing there—

I hear your inner voice;

I know you have dreams, and you're nervous.

Don't worry.

I will match your fear with my calm.

I will match your tears with empathy.

We will make a plan—together,

 cultivating kindness and confidence each day.

Because I am your coach,

I trust and believe in patience.

I will motivate you and show you respect in every way.

Let's promise to cheer for each other and be grateful.

And I will promise to be in tune with your desires

and safety.

I will honor you, and all your feelings,

even if I don't understand

because I value integrity.

And I see you, standing there,

I hear your voice,

and you matter.

CHAPTER 6

I Will Teach You

Find heroes and inspiration, teach from your heart,
and always, from the wisdom inside of you.

The Thrill

Victory! "The thrill of victory! And the agony of defeat...." I was a kid and heard those famous lines at the beginning of every *Wide World of Sports* TV show. I saw the most talented, brave, and unrelenting athletes around the globe: skiing, cycling, weight-lifting! They'd perform a mind-blowing feat and I was hooked—*hooked!*

ABC Sports must have known there is a psychology to what viewers will watch. Seeing those athletes didn't just grab my attention, it taught me a lot about my ambition. I wanted to be just like them, strong, wild, and *gutsy*.

So...do you know what stirs your athletes? How do you hook them? Do you know what challenges they like? Watch how athletes listen, behave, and respond to your words and ideas. Watch closely. Because the shy one may speak up. The funny one may be the star. And the driven child—who does all the conditioning and then some—will be very self-critical. Think about your athletes: what grabs their attention and makes them want to do more? Let's look at how athletes *learn*.

I've Never Coached Before

At the first team meeting, I had my 7th and 8th grade basketball team fill out a short questionnaire. I wanted to get to know them and find out what they wanted to achieve. I told them that I'd had a lot of success in sports, as a gymnast and a gymnastics coach. I won many national championships (they smiled and listened closely), and then I added that I'd never played or coached basketball before… And the room got still. Then I said, "I'll be honest. I'm scared. Because I want to win, and I want to be the best coach for *you*."

That season we worked hard, I got down and did crunches and push-ups with them—we joked, laughed, and boy, did they run a lot. Teen-age girls with red cheeks, sweat dripping down, and completely out of breath. I taught them to be "mean" girls on the court, how to protect the ball, and how to visualize their shots and plays. They practiced with true commitment, and they evolved. By the end of the season, playing many tough teams, these girls, who bordered on average talent, won the NJB Division Championship. I was amazed. The group bond between them, and the trust they had in me, were our strongest assets. I believe it began with that first team meeting. I said I was scared… and I taught them it was okay, and that they, too, could overcome their fears.

Do not hold back when something is real and could be an emotional touchstone. Make the human connection. Because coaching well is more about inspiring your athletes than teaching a skill. Inspire your athletes with honesty and care, and you will be teaching them much more than how to be great athletes. They will become great people.

The psychology of learning is not about teaching skills; it's about the inner person and what makes them tick. Pay attention, coaches, and make sure to get some guts. This journey is only for the real and the brave.

Rule #1

"Come on in! Sit down!" said Jack, his broad smile lifted his cheeks.

We walked into his office, and he sat in an executive leather chair that swiveled side to side. Behind a large dark wood desk, Jack was a balding, short man, stocky and strong with a bit of a belly. He wore a blue polo shirt and black, Clark Kent glasses. On my right, a grand bookcase stood with many books. My mom and I sat in two visitor chairs in the middle of the room. On my left, there were plaques on the wall. My mom had just signed me up at a nationally respected gymnastics club in California, and we came to meet with Jack, the owner and head coach.

I was quiet as Jack and my mom spoke about the team, the practice schedule, and parent involvement. Jack had a powerful presence, every word stated directly. He was about structure, rules, and discipline. Which I was used to. At home, there were a lot of rules to keep a tidy house and raise well-mannered children. There were seven kids in my family, and we all sat around the dinner table every night. My dad reminded us, "Sit up straight, both feet on the floor, and no elbows on the table."

I listened to Jack talk, and I was curious about him as my new coach. He had a spirit that vibrated and a hearty laugh. Yet there in his office, there was no doubt he was the chief. One plaque on his wall told you that—it read:

COACH'S RULES

RULE #1
THE BOSS IS ALWAYS RIGHT.

RULE #2
IF THE BOSS IS WRONG, REFER TO RULE #1.

Okay, at least he had a sense of humor.

For the past five years, I had trained and competed for a small club. But I had seen Jack's army of gymnasts at meets—they stood up straight in rows, their hair combed and sprayed perfectly in ponytails with white ribbons. They wore royal blue sweats with red and white stripes running down the sides: the colors of the American flag. Even though they were gymnasts and smiled a lot, they appeared to be confident soldiers, ready to kick your butt.

My mom and Jack chatted on for a while. Suddenly, Jack caught my attention.

"Does she *eat?*" he asked my mom, right as I sat there.

"Yes, she does." My mom grinned.

Then Jack grinned at me, like he was excited to get into the gym and start coaching me at that moment.

I was a tough, skinny, thirteen-year-old kid, five feet tall, flat chested, and eighty-five pounds. My hair was short and curly; I had braces on my teeth, and I was often mistaken for a boy. I was never a "girly-girl" and didn't want to be. In sports and in my family, you got attention for working hard, going after goals, and being determined and resilient. In my mind, nothing else was more important. I mean, I was aiming to compete in the Olympics, so being tough was precisely my everyday goal.

Then Jack looked at my mom and said, "She's going to work hard, and in a year, she'll be in the top three at our gym." That sounded crazy. They had a big team, including a group of Elite gymnasts, and a few on the U.S. National Team. Even though I was just one level below, I felt like a rookie in comparison.

I began to train with the team, five nights a week: 6:00-9:30 at night, plus Saturday mornings. There were fifty gymnasts on the floor doing acrobatic drills, going across in rows, up and down the floor. Jack yelled, "Round-offs! Go!" and a row of girls tumbled across the floor. "Go!" Jack yelled to the second row, and they rushed across. "Go!" he repeated, "Go!" he said again. Athletes ran, punched, and flipped one after another. I watched and followed along. I tried my hardest: I ran fast, grit my teeth, and jumped as high as I could. Sure, I kept up, I did the numbers, but my performance, I thought, was marginal. I wanted to be one of the best. I wanted the coaches to look at me, nod, and say, "Good job, Mitzel. Good job."

That's what I wanted.

But a determined athlete has rules, too…and they go like this:

```
┌─────────────────────────────────────┐
│   ATHLETE'S RULES                    │
├──────────────────────────────────────
│  RULE #1                             │
│     BE TOUGH—NO MATTER WHAT.         │
│  RULE #2                             │
│     IF YOU FEEL UNSURE,              │
│     WEAK, OR ABOUT TO CRY,           │
│     REFER TO RULE #1.                │
└─────────────────────────────────────┘
```

That first year was incredible. I got to compete in the U.S. Team Nationals with my teammates and we won. We were the #1 team in the country. I was only fourteen years old and felt like I was in the big leagues. Nothing prepared me like the hard work in the gym—even after a competition. There were times when we returned to the gym at 9:00 p.m., after an all-day meet, and Jack was angry that we had "too many mistakes." So, he told the parents to wait while we had to hit 10 out of 10 back-flips or side aerials on beam. No falls allowed. This could take up to an hour, and the intensity was insane. Girls tried. We'd make six, but then on seven, someone wobbled and fell. Jack hollered, "Start over!" You weren't supposed to look around, but I saw tears. I heard sniffles. There was no talking. I had to focus on my next turn.

I tell ya, I learned how to suck it up. I learned how to let go of worry and frustration and simply focus on the task. I was transforming: I had joined the ranks in being a soldier.

As I began my second year of training under Jack and his staff, I cultivated a sharper inner edge. The serious tone for achievement every day prefaced my workouts. I got sucked in and I loved it. I was both excited and nervous in the car on the way to practice, which often showed up as a stomach ache. When coaches yelled, it was about tasks and effort—but sometimes it was personal. Ultimately, I got a rush out of the hard assignments and orders because I liked being pushed. I didn't doubt for a second that they cared for me; it was simply a regimented program. But the coaches were friendly, they cracked jokes, and we all laughed plenty. I got hugs and pats on the back for successes and trying my best. Sure enough, I was in the top three right after the one-year mark. I had risen, and I realized, Jack was not only strict, but smart. He knew how to train athletes, and maybe, maybe he really knew me. He was the boss, and every day I was compelled to fight and do what it took. I liked the rules. They shaped my courage and my dreams…and I wanted more.

Understand the Message: I had a 'boss coach' who was also smart, funny, and cared for us. The structure was great, and the "rules" worked for my personality and in that era. But it's not for today. The moral to this story is the psychology of coaching is evolving. We must consider individual athletes. I was off-the-charts determined; most are not. To care for and protect, we must understand *how to teach each athlete*. Take some time to seek wisdom.

Learning is Cool

I was a labor-loving athlete. I loved the training process, and I also loved competing. For my temperament and goals, I was lucky to have coaches who pushed us to be our best; but truly they emphasized that hard work was the *greatest journey*. Many of us are way too attached to winning. Winning is fun, of course. I want to win all the time. But as a community, we are way too serious about it and desperate for it. Of course, we all want our athletes to do well. We ask them after a game, "Did you win?" "What was the score?" and "Where did you place?" I know, I know, when my kids were young, I was brainwashed, too, and I did that. Sheesh! But I became aware. I woke up. I learned that the questions to ask are, "Did you have fun?" or "What happened at the game?" or "What went well?" When we focus on results and awards, it feels like pressure and judgment for the athlete.

A mindset of 'results' sucks the joy out of learning.

But, we can shift our thinking to being curious, try new drills and new perspectives, *because learning is cool!* Seek to know the inner athlete, their personalities and desires, and be their partner. The best part of coaching, for me, is to connect with my athletes, and see what we can do *together*. Winning is the rare eagle in the sky: it's up there, soaring, and some days we actually get to see it. But guiding an athlete's mind, body, and spirit on a daily basis is the beautiful butterfly, a symbol of grace and transformation. Don't you think? Treasure *that*. And consider that sport is more fabulous when we connect on the inside.

Sport is Intellectual

Wisdom tells us there is a lot to examine and understand in sports.

To teach athletes at every level how to be in tune with their body and how to win takes a thousand steps before the day of competition, and we need to walk it together.

Coaches, parents, and athletes, we are lucky to come together to learn, improve, and enjoy the challenges competition brings. Sports can build character when you seek it and facilitate it. Education is what we're here for. Education and the habit of making healthy choices, these are lifelong practices. Wisdom makes us better for our athletes... and the world.

Psychology of Learning

The Psychology of Learning is wayyy more than giving and following instructions. It's *how we learn*. Not *what* we learn. When you're open to different approaches, make sure to include the *human calculation* and *human connection*. Consider the way *an athlete's mind works*. If you ever took psychology courses in school, you're ready! Because I'm going to borrow, simplify, and apply the nerdy stuff to sports. It's easy! Next, are three types of learning. When you grasp these styles, you can vary team practices and *choose* how to motivate and *increase* the learning rate in a smart, positive manner:

1. **Association:** Like Pavlov's dog, a bell rings, then food arrives. After repetitions of the same pattern, the dog is conditioned with a response and salivates at the ringing bell, knowing the food is coming. For athletes, arriving at a competition often produces nerves. But if you create a "fun competition activity," like taking silly photos or stretch to rockin' warm-up music, they will look forward to it! Tell your athletes first, before they do the "fun activity," to put their sports bag on a chair. After a number of competitions, placing their bags down in an organized manner will be familiar, and they will be conditioned. They'll know what's coming next

and actually start to feel excited *before* they put down their bag. The pattern becomes "normal," a new "routine" has been set, and nervousness will decrease.

2. **Consequence:** When an athlete makes a great play or nails a skill, it feels awesome; everyone cheers, and the coach gives high-fives. The athlete gets an endorphin high and is "hero" for the day. Positive consequences are effective and build self-esteem. On the other side, we can use punishment for mistakes or attitudes, like harder conditioning or sitting out as a repercussion. Athletes may respond, but some will shut down. Over time, the negative emotions that follow *punishment* become a pattern of fear and feeling inadequate. Be a teacher, not a punisher, and be wise! Use positive consequences as much as possible.

3. **Observational:** Just like me as a kid, watching *Wide World of Sports*, this is the most natural form of learning—by watching, getting inspired, then imitating. It's exciting to watch and imagine doing a task, movement, or skill. And it's self-motivating.

Come up with three different tasks for your team. Mix it up! Be inventive and fun with your athletes. You will teach them to be curious and embrace new ideas!

Wise Coaches Use Mindfulness

Wise and successful coaches often take pause when they reflect. They recognize they don't know *everything* because sport is a lot of trial and error, and there's a continual path of learning. The fear we fear is being judged. We may even chase success to appear smart! Growing in wisdom means you practice pausing and using mindfulness.

Mindfulness is to put your attention on personal experiences, moment-by-moment, accepting them without judging "good" or "bad."

Coaching with mindfulness consists of more patience, noticing the self, and less pushing the athlete. Mindful coaching is more personal and very meaningful in developing yourself.

In a practice, notice if you feel it's task, task, task. And bodies running, kicking, and jumping. It can become a blur of activity. When you're about to give feedback to an athlete and your knee-jerk reaction is to be quick and critical to keep up the pace, instead, pause… Pause some more…coach the *person* and be *mindful*…

Magical Tips to being Mindful with Athletes

- Take a deep breath before speaking (take a breath, now)
- Think about this one athlete
- Who are they as a person and how can I help?
- What's going on underneath the surface?
- What do you want to say—while keeping the athlete's spirit in mind?

Take a breath, again…release any muscle tension…pay attention to your body in this moment. You are practicing slowing down. This may sound ridiculous in an action-oriented practice. But if you don't slow down and make a change, you can't make a change! Model mindfulness to your athletes. Apply the humanistic approach. We want athletes to learn this, and we want to teach the athlete, not the skill. To make a real impact, do it by being *mindful*.

Exercises:

Focus On

To be mindful, focus your thoughts on these things...

1. the athlete's unique personality

2. what they did well, no matter how small

3. inner strengths, character

4. their effort at practice or a game and trying their best

Be Attentive

To be mindful, put your attention on...

1. the athlete's goals and desires

2. their physical and mental strengths and areas to improve

3. their struggles and challenges and how you can encourage and strategize together

4. a plan to get calm with the athlete, problem solve and adjust

It takes pause and reflection to be mindful and teach effectively. You may have habits—trying to motivate or fix problems with quick flashes of "try harder," or "just do it." But these are vague statements and are not always helpful. Let's inspire kids and get excited about learning! Take steps to evolve your coaching style. You can add more tools to your tool kit and embark on a new journey with your athletes as partners.

Self-efficacy Boosts Intelligence

How often do you ask an athlete: *What do you think?*

Coach: "We're going to do ten pushups, five times. That's fifty, total. It will be tough, but we'll do it one set at a time: you will get stronger, and I think you can do it. What do you think, can you do it?"

You're really asking your athletes, "Do you believe you can do it?"

Self-efficacy is the athlete's belief in their own ability to succeed in a certain situation—to make it through conditioning, perform a skill, or do well under pressure.

Teaching self-efficacy is super powerful, especially when you ask, "Do you believe you can?" To be clear, it's not the coach's or parent's belief, but their own belief that is imperative. Your belief helps. But in order to increase self-efficacy, a young person needs ongoing, positive encouragement, regular practice in organizing their thoughts, frequent little successes, and actively participating in the planning stages to reach goals.

An Athlete's Confidence Grows Through:

1. expressing *their* thoughts,

2. interacting with coaches using *their own* voice,

3. and asserting themselves through steps that *they* control.

4. Never feeling forced but stimulated to assert *their own* volition to participate and achieve.

Your approach is to help *athletes* think...process how *they* will perform...allow them to speak up and strategize with you...what will *they* do mentally and physically...?

Next, through a type of dialogue, see how athletes can feel more in charge of themselves, develop self-efficacy, and feel intelligent.

Coach-Athlete Dialogue: Ask Questions, Focus on Specifics, and Develop Self-efficacy

Coach: *We're going to do 5 laps as fast as you can. Think about your own time, not others. How fast do you want to go? Can you increase your speed?*

Athlete: *Yes! I can!*

Coach: *What will you do to improve your speed?*

Athlete: *Better technique. I'll focus on my positions and correct my moves.*

Coach: *Can you get specific? Exactly, what will your body do? Will you stretch your hand or arm in a straight line? Will you kick harder or faster?*

Athlete: *I will reach farther with my arms.*

Coach: *Great. Good strategy. And who will take a deep breath and talk to themselves?*

Athlete: *I will!*

Coach: *Super. I will watch, and you can show me.*

Build Confidence: Focus on Inner Strengths!

I often get asked, *"How do you build confidence? I have a kid who is scared, gives up easily, and is just not confident."* Remember the list of "Essential Needs for Athletes" in Chapter 3? Let's review: Person-centered is #1. Effort and Strengths is #2. Coaches and parents will typically focus on muscular strength, speed, agility, skills, or game strategy. All physically related—because this is sports! But may I remind you—even though athletes benefit from detailed instruction on the body's positions, movement, and fitness, there is great reason for a balance between the skills and guiding the person.

---

*Athletes **need** emotional fuel and human connection. They need to know they are smart, appreciated, and they have value—that gives them confidence! Focus on inner strengths and effort.*

That's imperative to being able to perform and advance physically.

Here are a few facts and ideas to spark your focus on your athlete's inner strengths.

1. **Harvard University:** Harvard has a class that's the most popular on campus, called Psychology 1504: Positive Psychology. They've studied people's strengths, skills, and talents. Skills are practiced and learned. Talent is innate. Strengths, on the other hand, relate to our natural capacity to behave, think, and feel in a way that is most authentic. For example, a natural capacity for laughter or light-hearted behavior; organizing ideas and people; demonstrating leadership by encouraging teammates. Each athlete is unique. When an athlete is acknowledged for and in tune with their strengths—and uses them frequently—they will have more desire to improve them *and even develop new ones.* Alternatively, when an athlete is disconnected from their strengths and doesn't use them, they will exhibit sadness, feeling lost, and their strengths begin to recede. Focus on inner strengths.

2. **Superheroes:** Most young people get excited about and even aspire to be like superheroes: Wonder Woman, Batman, Flash, The Black Panther. To increase focus and confidence, I am both playful and intentional and I encourage using *mental powers!* Consider people and characters who are revered for their wisdom or kindness. Look for moral exemplars, like Athena, the Greek goddess known for wisdom. She's a goddess, a warrior, and she's often seen with an owl. For that reason, owls are a symbol of wisdom and intelligence. I bring a little stuffed owl (I named her Athena), to  clinics and trainings. I say to athletes, "You are very wise," and touch Athena to their head or shoulder. Oh my gosh, athletes love this. They become charged with energy, and they focus *more* on their thoughts and their inner strength.

3. **"I am learning to compete!"** — Competing well is a skill. A mental skill. When you take away the attention from results, scores, and winning titles (all external items), you are releasing a lot of pressure. And instead, talk about the inner skills, how to get calm, what to focus on, and how to compete. Athletes will pay more attention to their mindset, and they will more easily grasp that they are in process and that they will improve. Practice looking forward with incredible belief. As athletes develop inner skills, they gain inner confidence because they know they have "it" inside of them.

Best of the Best

As a coach at Stanford University, I was very lucky! Where Stanford teams have won over 115 National titles, I learned from the "best of the best" that constant education and discussion with peers are important and necessary. I attended monthly department meetings with all coaches in every sport. At Stanford, professional development was our lifestyle. It was a frequent practice, discussion, and thoughtful follow-through. About a hundred coaches, including Olympic champions, world champions, and legends participated in these meetings: Richard Quick (swimming), Dick Gould (tennis), Bill Walsh (football) and Tara Vanderveer (basketball) were just a few. These coaches were the finest in the U.S. and the world, and yet they were still learning. They were also our teachers. The blend of older and younger coaches only added to the conversation and truly opened minds. Listening to them talk triggered me to ask questions and think deeper about how to improve myself, my athletes' motivation, conditioning, or what to ask sports doctors regarding injuries. I loved it, and I went home each night thinking more about trying new things to help my team. It was hard to go to sleep! I was constantly inspired.

Make a lifestyle and a friend of education. It's a modest practice because no one knows everything. My message to you? Always be curious, seek information, and be very, very humble.

How We Begin to Change

Alrighty, friends, it's true! You can cultivate higher ideals. And "change" requires ongoing effort and transformation. When we all seek education and transformation, we are beginning to create a safer environment and more dynamic culture for athletes. The first step is you... You've been reading about self-awareness, going deep, and connecting with athletes. Now, sit...and start with yourself...

- Sit with great humility and admit you probably need to learn new thoughts and ideas.

- Talk to others who want to change, take action-steps and be accountable to ensure a real transition will occur.

- Release any need to judge: you are in process, others are in their process.

Wake up every morning and decide to be open, "I am curious today. Who will I meet? Who will I talk to? What will I learn?" It takes at least 60 days of consecutive practice to create new habits. As you take personal stock and decide that you're *seriously on board* to becoming a partner to athletes, you can start viewing the athlete as a complex human being. You can practice saying this, "Hello, young athletes—I see you are humans! You have thoughts and feelings and different personalities. I am curious. And I care. Let's work together!"

Ladies and gentlemen, in coaching and parenting, you can now use the "Humanistic Approach." Remember to trust the universe. Do not judge. Be in the present moment. And inspire!

CHAPTER 7

I Believe in You

Don't give up. I believe in you all.
Athletes are powerful, no matter how small!

Belief. An athlete shows self-belief when they start to see their dreams are possible. When we teach mental skills, how to use inner powers, and we believe in a young person, their dreams are right there. Because they learn to believe in themselves.

Teach the Power of the Mind

In 100% of my mental training sessions with athletes, every single one of them says, *"I want to feel more confident and in control."* "Confident" is what all athletes want to feel. But it is learned, it doesn't come from nowhere. Confidence is a practice. So, line up your team and begin!

These three mental processes,

1. Mental Training

2. Mindfulness

3. Positive Psychology

…have proven that human beings can acquire great self-awareness and be able to keenly focus on a task with ease and *pure confidence*. We've already covered Positive Psychology in Chapter 3, and Mindfulness in Chapter 6, now it's time for Mental Training!

Mental Training Makes the Difference in Safety

Through mental training, coaches and parents can help athletes de-stress, make wise choices, and use the power of their mind to feel great and perform their best. To be clear:

Mental Training is not just to overcome nerves or im-prove performance…it's also for **safety.** *Through mental training, athletes will feel safer in playing sports and safer with people.*

When athletes are mentally connected to their thoughts and feelings, they become more in charge of themselves. They become more aware of details in movement, their emotions coming and going, and they feel more intelligent. The best part, in terms of safety, athletes are able to make wiser decisions based on their comfort and inner process—they can decide what feels *right* and *not right.*

Teach athletes *how to be in tune and understand their thoughts and emotions,* **and they will:**

- be able to manage nervousness and anxiety,
- perform more accurately, consistently, and confidently,
- develop a stronger sense of self and their values,
- form a deeper trust for the training process,
- identify negative and hurtful behaviors and be more likely to seek help when needed.

The Six Mental Skills: Self-Knowledge and Inner Power

There are six basic Mental Skills that serve as a strong foundation in all sports to manage thoughts, emotions, self-awareness and behaviors. When coaches talk about and facilitate regular practice of mental training, it's truly inspiring for athletes! I have found that nearly every one of my clients reports back that they feel more optimistic and confident after practicing and applying the mental skills. They'll do it for 30-seconds before they take a turn or make a play, or for 5-10 minutes at the end of practice, or especially at night in bed, before sleep. Talk about Mental Skills, put up posters about mental training! Facilitate brief practice for your athletes, because these are simple tools that are incredibly powerful. They turn anxiety into calm, confusion into clarity, and doubt into confidence.

The Six Mental Skills

1. **Breathing** - intentionally inhale and exhale, f-u-l-l-y, repeat several times and produce a centered, calm mental and physical state.

2. **Relaxing** - breathe into and release muscle tension to feel completely at ease.

3. **Positive Self-talk** - speak aloud or silently to yourself, using true positive statements, or repeat an optimistic script and create an inner confidence.

4. **Recall** - relive an action in detail, or flashback to a place or event, or remember a personal feeling or thought; see familiar mental images.

5. **Visualization** - dream or imagine a performance, see in your mind's eye a certain place or event, and envision, step-by-step, what you want to do!

6. **Concentration** - set your attention on one thing: sustain focus on one action at a time, taking your time; or focus on a central image or thought, even repeat the thought multiple times.

Coaches and athletes can work together to increase mental-emotional awareness. Athletes will learn to trust their abilities, speak positively to themselves, and play much better. It's important to have a clear intention to practice often, put it on your schedule, and learn to apply the skills in the right moment. Use the skills every day—in between turns and plays—to overcome problems and enhance moves. Weave in visualizing a skill, suggest positive self-talk before their next turn instead of thinking about a correction. To learn and teach details of how to practice these skills, check into my first book, *Focused and On Fire: The Athlete's Guide to Mental Training & Kicking Butt*. It is a companion book to *Focused and Inspired*. These books will help you include some type of mental training and safety, every day.

Exercise: A Moment of Confidence

One of the funnest exercises is to have your athletes line up in front of a mirror, or gather in a circle, and shout out, "I'm terrific! I'm terrific! I'm terrific!" (three times). Clap and laugh—it's super fun. This is mental training, no doubt about it! This exercise can be successful to develop energy for physical training, a positive bond with you and your team, and a strong inner voice and good feelings, when done frequently.

Patterns and Rhythms of Threes

1, 2, 3. On your mark, get set, go! Push, push, push! These are rhythmic norms in sports. In life, we have them, too! For instance: morning, noon, and night. Breakfast, lunch, and dinner. Before, during, after. High, medium, low. Big, bigger, biggest! There are probably thousands.

When you use patterns and rhythms of three, you literally click into a comfortable and soothing cadence.

Patterns are normal for all of us, and when a word or phrase is repeated 3 times, we remember it, it becomes more familiar, and it's easier to apply in sports!

From our childhood, think of nursery rhymes and songs, notice the repetitions and accents in threes: *Mary had a little lamb.* Or *Row, row, row your boat.* These are calming and pleasant songs that have the rhythm of three. As human beings, we click into a happy feeling or gratifying feeling when we experience this pattern.

Incorporate this magical repetition and comforting strategy—say things three times, like:

I am calm,

I am calm,

I am calm.

Tell your team:

You are brave, you are brave, YOU ARE BRAVE!

They will love it, and truly, athletes will remember the message much better. They will use it. And they will concentrate and feel more confident.

Exercise: Think It, Write It, Say It - Three Times!

When you communicate with yourself in 3 different ways, you create inner strength. Write three phrases that you want to teach your athletes. For instance: *I am in tune with my body.* or *I am fast!* or *We work hard.* Whatever message you believe is positive and important. They will think it, write it, and then say it. So ask them to repeat each phrase three times—as a group or separately, but loud enough so they hear their own voice. The repetitions can literally shift and elevate their personal power. Do this each day for a week! See what happens!

1. _____

2. _____

3. _____

And always make it fun—tell them they're growing big, strong mental powers!

The Benefits of Mental Training for Performance

When athletes learn and practice mental skills, the benefits are:

- Acute awareness of thoughts, breath, and body;

- The capacity for deep focus, shutting out all distractions;

- The aptitude to slow down the mind, reduce stress and overcome struggles;

- Accuracy and consistency in performances;

- The habit of creating a peaceful, confident feeling inside, even under pressure.

As athletes practice mental skills, they'll be able to *distinguish* between feeling calm and nervous. They will *execute* well in the most important moments. And they will *notice sooner* when they start to feel afraid, then manage it, or speak up and get help.

Talk About It: Fear is Normal

We mostly think of mental training and sport psychology to help athletes with their biggest challenges. But there are daily normal struggles, and it's a delicate balance for athletes to decide within themselves— "Should I be *tough* or be *real?*" In sports, they are directed, prodded, and pushed to be tough. The messages they keep receiving are, *Don't think about how you feel. Just ignore it and keep going!*

Most athletes try to keep going in a challenging moment, some give up sooner. But all kids try to be tough on some level. In 100% of my work as a coach and a mental training coach, every athlete is afraid to be called or judged as "weak."

I know this. Because they tell me. And I know it to my core as a former elite athlete. Now, in my role as a mental training coach, athletes hear my gentle voice and recognize that I'm a good listener. I'm very understanding, and *I never judge them*. They cry in front of me, cheeks get red, and tears spill out. Male athletes express heavy emotions and deep stress about being judged or ridiculed. All athletes tell me they feel so afraid of showing any of these emotions to their coach, sometimes their parents, and never want to show emotions at a practice. They are supposed to be tough. Especially guys, right? Boys aren't ever allowed to be "weak," and that is so sad and unhealthy. Faking has been the only way to cope. In fact, that has been a norm in sports. When I was a competitive athlete, we said it out loud, "Fake it till you make it!" and we were both proud of it and probably a little nervous. Understand and teach the difference in getting through a hard practice, or being hurt, worried or scared. Often boys hold it in so much for so long, they explode or break down in other ways, acting out physically or creating worse problems. Feelings are powerful. Emotions accumulate and build up in an unhealthy way, to the point that is damaging.

Regarding abuse, we want athletes to be *aware* of their emotions, and *aware* of their fear, so they notice when someone is mistreating them. If athletes stuff it down, then they ignore their true feelings. We need to talk and educate our young people about fear, nervousness, the signs of how you experience it in your mind and body, and what to do next. Let's talk about it.

Types of Fear

Athletes experience many fears. Some of them are:

1. Fear of tension / a stressful conversation

2. Fear of criticism / not being good enough

3. Fear of pain / getting injured or hurt

4. Fear of pressure and rejection by a coach or teammates

5. Fear of failure / not reaching your goal

6. Fear of not being an athlete / losing your identity

7. Fear of being in the wrong sport / not the right abilities

8. Fear of "wrong" body type / too heavy, short, tall, skinny

9. Fear of being judged that you have no value / you're nothing

Become Aware of the Signs of Fear

Quick question: What signs of fear or nervousness do *you* experience? When you react fast on the freeway to avoid a crash? When you can't find your wallet? When you have to answer a question to a police officer!

What do you *feel and experience in your body when scary or nerve-racking things happen? Because, when you are in tune with yourself, with your own fearful moments, you'll be able to understand more and empathize more with your athletes.*

Talk about it. Ask your athlete how he/she feels. They may not say a word, or say, *"I'm fine,"* so just stay cool around them. Relax. Because the fact is, they know you're okay to talk about fears. It's not voodoo!

So, if you can find out when their fear occurs, that can help you as a parent or coach in guiding them. I discuss these symptoms of fear openly in clinics. The athletes all share and we agree on what happens when we are scared and nervous. "Oh yeah, I get shaky," they say, or "My heart races," "I feel confused," or "I get sweaty." Athletes appreciate becoming more aware and learning that this is all very *normal!*

Understand the Body's Reaction to Fearful/Nervous Thoughts

- muscles tense up, feel shaky

- stomach aches badly/butterflies

- hair on arms and neck stand up

- goosebumps/chills

- sweaty hands/feet

- mind is confused, worried, panicky

- heart races

- sudden images of worst possible scenario

- emotions feel overwhelming, tears come, not able to talk or perform

Slow Down Everything

One simple method that is amazingly powerful...*slooowww down*. When athletes notice the signs of fear and nervousness, they can take steps to slow down... When a person pauses and slows down, it helps them to manage thoughts and emotions and be able to think more clearly. This conversation can be in the same tone of *how* to run faster, or *ways* to do proper technique on a drill or ab exercises. Talking about common fears is helpful!

Help Athletes Manage Feeling Scared:

When athletes start to feel afraid, tell them to...

1. Take a breath...

2. Let go of tension by relaxing your muscles

3. Drop your shoulders, loosen your jaw, let your hands and arms hang at your side

4. Say slowly, "I am calm...I am calm...I am calm...."

5. Feel your body soften and focus on your breath going in...and going out...

6. Talk to a trusted adult who can help you

After you practice with your athletes (yes, practice with them, pretty please) and they learn to do this exercise, brainstorm on *who* to talk to for more help. Maybe a coach, teammate, or parent. A team manager or team trainer. Talking is a start! Practicing these steps 2 or 3 times a week for several weeks creates higher awareness and a way to recognize stress, fear, and how to handle it.

For more information on this topic, you may read my companion book, *Focused and On Fire: The Athlete's Guide to Mental Training & Kicking Butt.*

Program the Mind with Powerful Mindsets

When positive and powerful mindsets are taught and held as major goals in training and competing—instead of scores or winning—athletes develop incredible inner strength, values, and a mature approach to handling challenges. In this section are eight powerful mindsets to practice! It's incredibly stimulating for athletes to learn these words and mindsets and apply them to sports. As young as seven-years-old, athletes love to feel smart. It gives them an emotional boost! Discuss and practice a mindset each week for eight weeks. Make it part of your team strategy to be mentally aware and prepared for competition. You are developing sharper minds and their "edge" for success!

1. **Volition** is the powerful will inside you that aims to rise up, take action, and perform well. It is an all-encompassing desire—a personal attitude that is developed through your vision of your future self. Watch a team movie with driven and determined athletes that inspires volition.

2. **Expectancy** is the quality or a state of looking forward or anticipating what's next, or what may come in the near future. If athletes feel great surprise, they were not prepared. It's important to be alert and ready to handle any situation. Give your athlete(s) a list of proper expectations for practices, handling injuries, travel guidelines, team philosophies, opponents, game venues, weather conditions, and competition protocol. There's even more, so teach them to expect and be ready for everything and anything. This is not the focus, this is simple preparation so they are not surprised.

3. **Present-moment Awareness** is being in-tune with your body's position, movement, and your thoughts and breath as it's happening. It's being focused on yourself, now: not in the past, not in the future, just what is happening with you right now.

4. **Mindfulness** is to put your attention on personal experiences, accepting them without judging "good" or "bad." Experience everything fully, watch your thoughts…your words…behaviors…just notice, and accept.

5. **Acceptance** is to permit the reality of a situation, especially something uncomfortable, not resisting or trying to change the present situation. To understand processes, know there are ups and downs; embrace reality and trust that things will be okay.

6. **Impermanence** is the understanding that everything in existence is temporary and transient. Things change and pass, lives constantly fluctuate and evolve. Nothing is permanent or forever enduring.

Newness always comes.

7. **Letting Go** is a practice in releasing a previous image, thought, or emotion; you can express and drop tension, discomfort, or fear. Then decide what's next: *I will adjust. I will heal. I will repair.* You can intentionally put mental clutter in the past, throw it in the trash, choose a new focus in the present moment, and move toward what you want.

8. **Resilience** is a personal choice to recover promptly from adversity. To rebound after setbacks, injuries, difficulties. You rise after a fall and bounce back after a mistake. You decide to refocus after confusion or failure. To be resilient is to make an intentional shift into positive thinking after a negative experience.

From my book, *Focused and On Fire*, this curriculum can be fun and inspiring. Make a sign with all of the Mindsets and post it somewhere the athletes can see it. Give examples, talk about it, inspire them, and ask your athletes to show you or tell you what they think. Then challenge them in a fun way to demonstrate a Mindset during practices. When they show it, cheer for them!

Visualizing Is like the Real Thing

Visualization, or imagery, is a guided mental practice, recalling or creating pictures in your mind, involving sensory details. Self-guided, or with someone prompting, you can get quiet and calm and recall an experience, a specific performance in the past, or imagine something in the future. It's more natural for athletes to recall mistakes and negative images—they do it all the time, believe me—but that's *not helpful*. Learn to create positive images, and when you involve muscular sensations, emotions, and your other senses, like sound, taste, touch, and smell, the image is very real.

Sport psychologists report that positive imagery arouses muscle response and emotions, like a real physical performance. Exact visualization is so similar to reality that your brain doesn't know the difference!

Training in imagery prepares you to play your best!

Your Brain is a Camera

You can encourage and even teach basics of how to visualize. Think of your brain functioning like a camera. A camera doesn't think. A camera doesn't talk or judge. It just sees. A camera takes a photo of an image, or a moving image, and your brain can do the same thing. When you hold a position for two seconds, and you pay attention to what you see and feel, "click!" your brain takes a mental "picture" of that position. You can do this in any sport, and the best place to start is with a basic move. Break down a simple move into parts. Then, let your mind be a camera. Notice and see your hands—see, they are in a *low* position (stop, look, and feel), medium position (stop, look, and feel), high position (stop, look, and feel). Like a sequence of still-shots, see each "picture" and position in your mind, and remember the sequence.

When you practice a mental sequence in s-l-o-w m-o-t-i-o-n, seeing through your mind's eye and feeling your body in each position, you are training mentally. You are imprinting exact movements in your mind: a master plan of what you will do. You can, at the very least, encourage your athletes, in between turns, to repeat their basic moves in their mind. This helps them to go *inward* and connect with themselves. And it helps with increasing concentration on step-by-step thinking, instead of focusing on results. Visualizing is very powerful.

Transform Through Positive Inner Work

Mental Skills can transform an athlete's performance.

Mental Skills can transform an athlete's self-confidence.

Mental Skills can transform an athlete's sports career.

Mental Skills can increase an athlete's overall safety.

Using mental skills has transformed *my entire life*. No kidding. I have used them in the smallest moments and the grandest occasions. I am in tune with myself, my calm inner voice, I visualize, and I feel capable of handling anything. You and your athletes will increase your self-awareness, and you'll enhance your abilities to face any challenge that arises. As a coach, parent, or if you're in a supportive role with athletes, you have incredible influence on them and their mental and emotional lives. Have fun teaching and encouraging these wonderful mental practices. They were gifts to me, and I know they will be gifts to you and your athletes.

CHAPTER 8

A Devotion and Epiphany

Guiding and support-ing an athlete is a gift; being in their lives, teaching, watching, helping them get up after a fall... But being involved with athletes is also strange and mysterious; we must release any personal at-tachment to their results. We, as coaches, can be the best ever, but success and winning relies on the athletes. We can be genius tech-nicians, and they may learn it, or they may not. They may do great in practices, and then falter in games. As parents, we cannot push or mold a young person to be the athlete we want them to be, even if it's our strongest desire. All of us together can only show up, be positive, and help them be who *they* want to be, because being an athlete is *their* desire. This is the athlete's journey. It's their story, not ours. We have chosen the sports world as part of our lives, and it's our absolute top priority to keep athletes safe and teach them ways—to physically and mentally—face challenges, get back up, and grow up as happy and healthy adults. Guiding an athlete is not about success. It is a devotion. And how blessed we are to connect and devote ourselves to precious young people. That sense of connection is a great responsibility, it's amazing, and I am forever grateful for that.

Gratitude is a guide for me in working with athletes. Often, I go walking for exercise, peace, and feelings of gratitude, and often it's at the beach. Recently, I was out walking with my dad, who is 80-years-young. We were passing a beach cafe, right on the sand. On a wall was a large, painted message he pointed out to me, "Lisa, have you read that?" No, I hadn't. We looked closer and it said: *If you're lucky enough to drink wine at the beach, you are lucky enough.* My dad laughed and I laughed, and we stood there and enjoyed being together, feeling grateful for the walk and the moment. We began strolling again, the ocean waves splashed onto the sand. Seconds later, a thought came to me. I said, "Dad, you know what that makes me think of...? Coaching... If you're lucky enough to coach...you're lucky enough." My dad stopped and we looked at each other.

A beach-walking epiphany.

For all of us, it is the greatest honor to be in the lives of athletes, to feel that incredible thrill of supporting, encouraging, and watching them reach new heights. Oh, what a gift! And after time goes by, after they've struggled and been hurt many times, if you cared for them, listened to them, and kept them safe, you may just get to watch them grow up, go out in the world, and do their magnificent things. And how wonderful and magical is that!?

Thank you for reading this book. Thank you for taking steps to change the culture of sports to a safer place for athletes. Let us all be well, walk in gratitude, and inspire human greatness.

Thank you...thank you...thank you...!

My Journey and Healing Resources

In this final section, there's a list of people and resources that have nurtured my spirit and influenced me immensely. I've been on a personal journey my whole life, seeking new goals and healing and growing from difficult challenges. As an athlete, I was tough and had incredible tunnel vision, which helped me overcome struggles, adversity, and attain certain achievements. In my adult life, I've faced more hardships, including abuse, illness, depression, divorce, and being a single mom. Amidst the pains, I've found peace inside myself when I needed it. I rise every time because of my beliefs, and the practice of self-awareness has truly been transformational. Reading books, listening to thought-provoking speakers, and continuing my education has added to my personal evolution. I now approach teaching with curiosity, gratitude, and wisdom. I'm a very patient and empathic coach, and I find deep connections with others. I express joy, determination, and incredible belief in the human spirit. I am blessed to the moon and back for all I've learned with great appreciation for higher learning at the University of Utah (BA Psychology), Spalding University (MFA in Writing), and with the astute and innova-

tive coaches I worked with at Stanford University. I am honored to share my knowledge and resources with you. My first book, *Focused and On Fire: The Athlete's Guide to Mental Training & Kicking Butt,* is a companion to this book, *Focused and Inspired.* I encourage you to read and share both books with everyone in the sports world and beyond. You can also find almost everything on my list online. Perhaps, you will continue to read, learn, and feel inspired even more...I hope you do!

Andre Agassi, athlete, author, *Open*

Dr. Maya Angelou, poet, singer, activist, author, poem "Still I Rise"

Dr. Brene Brown, research professor, author, speaker, TED Talk "The Power of Vulnerability," Video "Empathy"

Dr. Leo Buscaglia, speaker, professor, author, *Love*

Anthony de Mello, Jesuit priest, speaker, author, *Awareness: The Perils and Opportunities of Reality,* and *The Way to Love: The Last Meditations of Anthony de Mello*

Dr. Wayne Dyer, speaker, author, *The Power of Intention: Learning to Co-create Your World Your Way*

Patricia Evans, author, *The Verbally Abusive Relationship: How to Recognize it and How to Respond.*

Thich Naht Hanh, Buddhist monk, peace activist, author, *Peace is Every Step: The Path of Mindfulness in Everyday Life*

Dr. Keith Henschen, sport psychologist, author, *Don't Leave Your Mind Behind: The Mental Side of Performance*

Timothy Gallwey, author, *The Inner Game of Tennis: The Classic Guide to the Mental Side of Peak Performance*

Elizabeth Gilbert, author, *Eat, Pray, Love.* and *Big Magic: Creative Living Beyond Fear*

Phil Jackson, coach, author, *Sacred Hoops*

Yann Martel, author, *Life of Pi*

Diana Nyad, athlete, speaker, author, video, "Diana Nyad: Extreme Swimming with the World's Most Dangerous Jellyfish"

Dr. Ken Ravizza, sport psychologist, author, *Heads-Up Baseball: Playing the Game One Pitch at a Time*

Rumi, scholar, poet *The Guest House*

Dr. Barry Schwartz, professor, author, video, TED Talk, "The Loss of Wisdom"

Jim Thompson, author, *Positive Coaching* and other books. Positive Coaching Alliance

Bill Walsh, coach, author, *The Score Takes Care of Itself*

Alan Watts, philosopher, author, video, "The Story of the Chinese Farmer"

Oprah Winfrey, talk show host, philanthropist, speech/video, "Harry's Last Lecture at Stanford University"

Insight Meditation Center, Redwood City, CA

Spirit Rock Meditation Center, Woodacre, CA

Palm trees, sunshine, and California beaches, my spiritual place

A Tribute to Ken Ravizza
1948-2018

Trust the Process!

Photo: Angels Baseball

Ken Ravizza was magic. It's that simple. He believed in the power of all human spirit, and amidst your moment of angst or doubt, he somehow got you to believe in yours. I was introduced to Dr. Ken Ravizza when I was fifteen years old, while struggling with fears in gymnastics. Ken was the real deal, a PhD and a college professor at Cal State Fullerton. But he did not appear to be a doctor to me. He was very laid back, he taught yoga and worked with athletes. He sported thick wavy hair and a full beard, relaxed shoes, and worn jeans. He was just Ken. When he walked he strolled with an ease, he smiled wide and greeted you with, "Heyyyyyy, how ya doing?" Ken was complete joy. In all of the world, I could not have imagined a better person to help me with my fears. He committed time, energy, and taught me everything in mental training with great detail. He sat quietly and curiously and listened to my thought processes and encouraged me. I felt more patient with Ken nearby, and it worked. I overcame my struggles and was successful. Since then, I've used mental skills and Ken's example of patient control and inner power my whole life. To realize that my current work in mental training and emotional intelligence is directly connected to Ken's influence is mind-blowing.

For over forty years, Ken made that same huge impact throughout the sports and education world. Many of his athletes, students, and colleagues continually stayed in touch with him, collaborated with him, invited him to speak, and simply spent time to soak up his incredible spirit. For millions whose lives were touched by Ken, he was known as a sport psychology pioneer, creating one of the first applied sport psychology graduate training programs in the United States. He also "normalized" the practice of mental training and presented methods that leaned into a person-centered and holistic approach for competitive athletes. Especially in college and professional baseball, Ken sparked a transformation that sport psychology was not only helpful but necessary. His inspiring methods and his book, *Heads-Up Baseball: Playing the Game One Pitch at a Time* were instrumental in elevating players, teams, and winning major league championships. Ken was not traditional, he was unique. He was said to be the "Godfather of Sport Psychology." Wow. I was honored that Ken had the manuscript for this book, *Focused and Inspired*, and was preparing to endorse it. I not only had his blessing, but passionate support. I can only say that I am humbled to my core.

Ken, you will always be an amazing part of so many lives. Just thinking of you reminds me to get calm and take the deepest breaths (you were so good at that!). I feel a great sense of honor in passing on your humor and wisdom. Partly because I keep hearing your voice: *Leee-sahh! Trust the process!* And so I do...because you believed in me, and you trusted, and Ken, to so many of us, you made it all feel like *magic*.

Acknowledgements

This book was barely a seed in my mind in late 2017. Then in early 2018, all over the media and in every sport, the safety issue exploded. In conversations with coaches and parents, I knew I wanted to work on this book. I want to say, "Thank you!" to all of the athletes who shared their personal thoughts and feelings with me. Thank you to all of the parents and coaches who trusted me and spoke with me about this pursuit of education and keeping athletes safe. Your belief in me and your heartfelt support has kept me centered on helping everyone in the sports community through wisdom and inspiration!

During these past months while writing and traveling, my greatest support has been my parents, Jim and Lorie Mitzel, and staying with them in Southern California. I've been on the road for over a year with my first book, *Focused and On Fire*, and my life has literally transformed; I uprooted myself from Northern California to follow my dreams. In between my trips, I'm in a beautiful home with good food, loving parents, and regular walks at the beach—I am peaceful inside while taking this leap. 'Thank you' doesn't get close to expressing my gratitude, but thank you, Mom and Dad. I'm so happy we're sharing this magical journey together.

Regarding the serious process of writing and producing a book, it takes a tireless and fabulous team of people. I am eternally grateful for my kind and generous readers, whose astute feedback literally helped me shift this book from important to impactful: Katie Hadrovic, Lisa Chester Aquirre, Tracy Hughes, Julia Zanutta, and Steve Shepherd. For the powerful endorsements, and especially your faith in me and this critical message about safety: Ricardo Azevedo, Dr. Sally Harris, Scott Johnson, Marcia Frederick, Steve and Gaby Arkell, Jim Thompson, and Steve Kerr. I am humbled by you. And then, I could not get this book to feel and act as a real book without my savvy professional crew who labored with me and brought it to life: My edgy and loving editor, Vanessa Anderson, my patient dear friend and exquisite designer, Judi Eichler, and the super amazing cover designer, George Foster (who also suggested I ask some big names to support this book, which definitely got me to be brave!). And then there are these two guys…these intelligent and wonderful gentlemen: Dr. Jerry George, you are a gem of a friend and a class act in connecting me to the right people, and lending me your passionate spirit and beautiful, compelling words. Hand on my heart, thank you. And last but certainly not least, Dr. Roy Vartabedian, my publisher with endless support, encouragement, and energy…I am so glad you trusted and believed in me, and that your inner drive is on par with mine! I am thankful each day for all the hours you put in to produce this important safety education. You have stretched me to go deeper in the writing, and I am sincerely grateful that we are partners. This is just the beginning, and look what we're doing!

Finally, this book, *Focused and Inspired*, would not be here, now, without the village of friends and coaches across the country who ignited the enthusiasm in July 2017, and this past year, for my *Focused Tour*. You truly opened the door to my journey of traveling and speaking, and because of you, I am reassured this is a viable and important path. From California to Massachusetts, "Thank You!" Thank you for giving me a boost and supporting my tour and my book, *Focused and On Fire*. To the amazing sponsors who are so kind and jumped on board to support this book and the *Focused Tour* on Safety for 2018-19, "Thank you!" And to my many incredible friends who hosted me, cared for me, sipped wine with me, helped me move, and gave book parties in their homes, you are so generous and loving. I am lucky to have you in my life. Thank you everyone...you must know, you really must know, you are blessings on earth.

Thank you, Sponsors! Spread the Word and Promote Athlete Safety Education with the *Focused Tour!*

It's true that you, me, and everyone—we are all in this TOGETHER!

Would you like to add your voice to this vital mission to advocate for athlete safety and wellness in every sport? Our mission is to educate coaches, parents, and leaders in sports, and help athletes thrive through emotional awareness, it takes many people listening, sharing, and *teaching*.

Come and join the movement and your name will be added to these amazing people and organizations who stepped up to be sponsors. Their contributions helped to produce this inspiring book and will assist with costs related to the U.S. and International *Focused Tour*. With your help we can teach methods to identify and prevent abuse and create healthy training models for coaches, athletes, and parents. Participants will gain insight to the psychology of coaching, managing struggles, and how to practice empathy and emotional intelligence.

With the *Focused Tour* Lisa is excited to continue her travels for a year to institutions, programs, and sports clubs within the United States and Internationally. **We can keep athletes safe. We can increase success through positive partnerships and power balance. We can work together and make a change.**

We invite YOU to join us for Safety Education with the *Focused Tour!*

Visit *www.gofundme.com/athlete-safety-education-tour* and Add Your Name to Our Fabulous Sponsors!

- IGC, International Gymnastics Camp
- Foster Covers, Inc.
- U.S. Gymnastics Suppliers Association
- Flight School Gymnastics Center
- Redmond Gymnastics Academy
- Achievers Gymnastics Center
- Ricardo Azevedo, Olympic Water Polo Coach
- Snowflake Designs
- Bay Aerials Gymnastics
- Eric Will Gymnastics Center
- Mary Wright, Olympic Gymnastics Coach
- Theresa Kulikowski-Gillespie, International Gymnast
- Cheryl Vance, Taekwondo World Champ & International Gymnast

For donations of $50 or more, you will receive a copy of the *Focused and Inspired* book. Your name or your business/program name will be added to the *Focused Tour* materials and sponsorship announcements. For company sponsors, reach out to Lisa and her team on *LisaMitzel. com* or *www.gofundme.com/athlete-safety-education-tour.*

Our goal is to raise $50,000 for the first year of the education tour, as well as in-kind support, to supplement groups who are passionate about the safety education, but can't afford the expenses involved to bring the tour to their location. We're thrilled to have your participation. You make the difference! Thank you!

Author-Illustrator

Photo: David Gonzales

Lisa Mitzel's passion is to work with a deeper understanding of human behavior in performance environments. As a speaker, consultant, and writer, Lisa teaches emotional intelligence and self-awareness in sport to facilitate athlete wellness, safety, and success for all. Her impact is vital, centering on an intellectual, compassionate, and whole-person approach to achieving goals. Her philosophies are rooted in her family and spirituality.

Lisa grew up in Southern California with her mom, dad, and six siblings. There was a lot of playing, learning, dancing, and praying at the dinner table. At age eight she started gymnastics, and over ten years she won State, Regional, and National titles. Despite a terrible crash in the gym, and experiencing acute psychological fears, Lisa trained with a pioneering Sport Psychologist, Dr. Ken Ravizza, and became a 2-Time Jr. Olympic National Champion. She competed Elite and placed in the top 25 in the country.

Lisa received a full scholarship to the University of Utah, and with a highly-motivated team and regimented mental training, she became an NCAA 6-Time All-American, National Champion, and member of 4 NCAA National Championship Teams. She earned a BA in Psychology, and later, Lisa was inducted into the University of Utah Hall of Fame.

After college, she coached competitive gymnastics teams and was soon the assistant coach, then Head Coach for Women's Gymnastics at Stanford University. Lisa guided her team to success with many All-Americans, an NCAA National top-10 finish, and started a new era of winning at Stanford.

Lisa raised three children and earned an MFA in Writing at Spalding University. She wrote and produced a sports TV show, published a chapter in *Routledge Handbook of Applied Sport Psychology,* and is now the author of two books, including her first, *Focused and On Fire: The Athlete's Guide to Mental Training & Kicking Butt,* 2017. She lives in California and is excited to influence leaders in the sports world and enhance the athletic community through mindfulness and inspired learning. Find out more at *LisaMitzel.com.*